BIG BOOK
OF
CAMARO DATA
1967-1973

John R. Hooper

MBI Publishing Company

First published in 1995 by MBI Publishing Company, PO Box 1, 729 Prospect Avenue, Osceola, WI 54020-0001 USA.

MBI Publishing Company books are also available at discounts in bulk quantity for industrial or sales-promotional use. For details write to Special Sales Manager at Motorbooks International Wholesalers & Distributors, 729 Prospect Avenue, PO Box 1, Osceola, WI 54020-0001 USA.

Library of Congress Cataloging-in-Publication Data

Hooper, John R.
    Big book of Camaro data, 1967–1973/
    John R. Hooper.
        p. cm.
    Includes index.
    ISBN 0-87938-973-7
    1. Camaro automobile—Specifications.
    TL215.C33H663   1995
    629.222'2—dc20   94-39846

On the front cover: This 1969 Dover White and Hugger Orange Camaro SS396/350hp is a pace car replica. Owner Barry Poet did his own restoration. *Dan Lyons*

Printed and bound in the United States of America

Contents

Chapter 1   **1967 Camaro**   4

Chapter 2   **1968 Camaro**   24

Chapter 3   **1969 Camaro**   44

Chapter 4   **1970 Camaro**   72

Chapter 5   **1971 Camaro**   88

Chapter 6   **1972 Camaro**   118

Chapter 7   **1973 Camaro**   120

Appendix A **Paint and Trim Combinations**   134

Appendix B **Engine and Transmission Teams**   142

Appendix C **Miscellaneous Dated Parts**   151

              Index   159

Chapter 1

1967 Camaro

1967 Manufacturer's suggested retail price (MSRP) for base model Camaros

Model Number	Description	MSRP
12337	six-cylinder Sport Coupe	$2,466.00
12367	six-cylinder convertible	2,704.00
12437	eight-cylinder Sport Coupe	2,572.00
12467	eight-cylinder convertible	2,809.00

Note: Manufacturer's suggested retail price **(MSRP)** includes the factory delivery and handling charge (including federal excise tax) and recommended dealer delivery and handling charge. This price does not include transportation charges, state and local taxes, or any accessories or optional equipment that may be ordered.

Camaro Standard Equipment

Protective inner skirts at both front and rear wheel openings; flush-and-dry rocker panels; dual master cylinder brake system with warning light; padded instrument panel; padded sun visors; energy-absorbing steering column; energy-absorbing instrument panel with smooth contoured knobs and levers; lane-change feature incorporated in direction signal; inside day-night mirror with shatter-resistant vinyl-edged glass and breakaway support; soft, low profile window control knobs and coat hooks; seat belts front and rear with push-button buckles; front seat belt retractors; front seat shoulder belt anchors; passenger-guard door locks on all doors; folding front seat back latches; energy-absorbing steering wheel; thick-laminate windshield; dual-speed windshield wipers; windshield washer; reduced-glare instrument panel and windshield wiper arms and blades; safety door latches and hinges; outside rearview mirror; back-up lights; four-way hazard warning flasher; high-level ventilation system; built-in blended-air heater and defroster system; Magic Mirror acrylic lacquer finish; friction-type ventipanes; curved solid tempered plate glass side and rear windows; two-key lock system; weather-shielded key locks; push button-type outside door handles, color-keyed interior trim; scuff-resistant plastic cowl side panels with molded-in ventilator grilles; quality interior features and appointments; full-view instrument panel with instruments and controls; and locking glove compartment.

Consult authorized Chevrolet dealers or your Fleet Representative for information on accessories and extra cost of optional equipment not listed.

General Motors Corporation reserves the right to make changes at any time, without notice, in prices, colors, materials, equipment, accessories, specifications, and models, and to discontinue models.

Serial Numbers and Identification
Vehicle Identification Number (VIN)

Six-cylinder example:

Model	Model Year (1967)	Assembly Plant (Los Angeles)	Unit Number (25th unit)
12337	7	L	100025

Therefore: The 25th model built at Los Angeles would be serial number 123377L100025.

Eight-cylinder example:

Model	Model Year (1967)	Assembly Plant (Norwood)	Unit Number (26th unit)
12437	7	N	100026

The front end of a 1967 SS350.

Therefore: The 26th model built at Norwood would be serial number 124377N100026.

Assembly Plants

L - Los Angeles
N - Norwood
Starting unit number was 100001 and up at each plant, regardless of series.
Location: Stamped on plate attached to left front body hinge pillar (inside door jamb).

Basic Specifications

Overall Length, in.	184.7
Overall Width, in.	72.5
Overall Height, in.	51.4
Wheelbase, in.	108.0
Front Tread, in.	59.0
Rear Tread, in.	58.9
Curb Weight, lbs.	2910
Usable Trunk Area, cu. ft.	8.3
Fuel Capacity, gal.	18

Transmission Identification

Example: S7E01
S - Plant and Type Designation Plants
    S - Saginaw, three-speed
    R - Saginaw, four-speed
    P - Muncie, four-speed
    C - Cleveland, Powerglide
    T - Toledo, Powerglide
501D - Production Month and Date
    5 - May
    01 - 1st day
    D - Day shift
    N - Night shift

Location:
Three- and four-speeds are stamped on the right-hand side of the case in upper front corner.
Four-speeds are stamped on top right side of case.
Powerglides are stamped on right side of pan.

Engine Identification

Example: F 1210 LA
F - Flint (source designation)
1210 - Production Month and Date
    12 - December
    10 - 10th day
LA - Type Designation

Types:
230ci six-cylinder
    LA - Regular production engine, three-speed
    LE - Regular engine, Powerglide

250ci six-cylinder (RPO L22)
    LN - Optional engine, three- or four-speed
    FM - Optional engine, Powerglide

302ci eight-cylinder (RPO Z28)
    MO - Special engine, manual transmission
    MP - Special engine, manual transmission with A.I.R.

327ci eight-cylinder
    MA - Regular production, three- or four-speed, four-barrel carburetor
    ME - Regular engine, Powerglide

327ci eight-cylinder (RPO L30)
    MK - Optional engine, three- or four-speed, four-barrel carburetor
    MM - Optional engine, Powerglide

350ci eight-cylinder (RPO L48)
    MS - Optional engine, three- or four-speed, four-barrel carburetor
    MU - Optional engine, Powerglide

396ci eight-cylinder (RPO L35)
    MW - Optional engine, three- or four-speed, four-barrel carburetor
    MY - Optional engine, Turbo Hydra-matic

Six-cylinder models are stamped on pad on right side of cylinder block to rear of distributor. Eight-cylinder models are stamped on pad at front right side of cylinder block.

Rear Axle Identification

Example: PW 0212 B
PW - Type Designation
    PW - 2.73, three- or four-speed and Powerglide
    QL - 3.31, RPO L48 three- or four-speed and Powerglide

    QT - 2.73, RPO L35 Turbo Hydra-matic
0212 - Production Month and Date
    02 - February
    12 - 12th day
B - Source Designation
    B - Buffalo
    G - Gear & Axle Plant
    W - Warren
Location: On bottom left or right of axle tube next to carrier housing.

1967 Camaro Regular Equipment— Exterior
Bright Metal Trim and Moldings

Stainless Steel

Back window reveal molding	coupe only
Belt molding rear	convertible only
Hubcaps	all
Windshield reveal molding	all
Windshield pillar molding	convertible only

Anodized Aluminum

Body sill molding - slender	all
Grill mounted headlight bezels - single unit	all
Radiator grill opening molding	all

Chrome-Plated Metal

Fender series emblem - Camaro	all
Front door vent window frame assembly	all
Front door vent channel and post	all
Front fender engine emblem (V-8 and optional 6)	all
Front header panel emblem - Chevrolet Camaro	all
Outside left-hand rearview mirror	all
Radiator grill emblem	all
Rear deck lid nameplate - Chevrolet Camaro	all
Rear quarter glass channel - front	all
Taillight bezels	all

Other

Back-up lamps	all
Black plastic radiator grill	all
Grill-mounted parking lights	all
Gas filler cap - rear end panel	all
Rear license lamp	all
Windshield wipers	
Two-speed with washer and satin-chrome hardware	all

The Rally Wheel found on 1967-69 Camaros.

Optional locking gas cap available on 1967-68 Camaros.

Bumper guard option for 1967-68 Camaros.

1967 Camaro Regular Equipment— Interior

Bright Metal Trim and Moldings

Armrest front door—bright base	all
Door and window control handles—colored plastic knobs	all
Door sill plates	all
Rearview mirror day-night padded frame w/bright breakaway support	all
Seat adjuster handle and front seat back lock handles - bright	all
Sunshade supports - bright	all
Windshield header molding - bright	convertible only

Instrument Panel

Ashtray and cigarette lighter	all
Control knobs - chrome "mushroom" type	all
Courtesy lamps	convertible only
Glovebox lock and interior lamp	all
Ignition lock and starter switch, "four-position"	all
Instrument cluster bezel and black texture trim plate	all
Brake system failure indicator, parking brake alarm	all

Other

Roof center dome lamp	coupe only
Steering wheel, three-spoke, horn button	all
Vent control knobs - colored plastic	all
Coat hooks (two) - soft colored plastic	coupe only
Door lock button, painted	all
Four-way hazard flasher	all
Freeway lane change signal	all
Heater - deluxe	all
Luggage compartment spatter paint	all
Padded instrument panel and sunshades	all
Passenger compartment floor covering - carpet	all
Rear armrest with ashtrays	convertible only
Seat belts, push button front and rear seats	all
Seats, front bucket	all
Switch, front door jamb	all
Ventipanes - friction type front	all

1967 Camaro Options and Accessories

When Factory Installed

V-8 Models (210hp Turbo-Fire 327 V-8)

12437	Sport Coupe	$2,572.00
12467	Convertible	2,809.00

Six-cylinder Model (140hp Turbo-Thrift 230 Six)

12337	Sport Coupe	2,466.00
12367	Convertible	2,704.00

Model Options

Z87

Custom interior: Includes color-keyed accent bands on seats, molded front door armrests with recessed door handles, glove compartment light, molded luggage compartment mat, and deluxe-styled steering wheel. Also includes roof sail panel lamps, rear armrests with ashtray on Sport Coupe model $94.80

L48

SS 350: Includes 295hp Turbo-Fire 350 engine, special hood and ornaments, front header panel paint stripes, special nylon red stripe tires, 14x6 wheels, fender "SS" emblems and "SS350" emblems on radiator grille, steering wheel hub, and gas filler cap $210.65

Z22

Rally Sport: Includes front valance-mounted parking lights, electrically operated headlight panels, body lower side moldings, body side accent stripes, front and rear wheel opening moldings, roof drip gutter moldings (Sport Coupe only), rear valance-mounted back-up lights, special grille styling and "RS" emblems on radiator grille, fender, steering wheel hub and gas filler cap $105.35

Style Trim Group: Included with Rally Sport option. Includes body side accent stripes, front and rear wheel opening moldings.

Z21   Convertible $29.50

Z21

Sport Coupe also includes bright roof drip gutter moldings $40.05

. .Special Interior Group: Includes bright trimmed pedal pads and bright windshield pillar moldings.

Z23   Convertible $5.30

Z23

Sport Coupe, also includes bright roof rail moldings $10.55

L35

Camaro SS: Includes special hood and ornaments, front header panel paint stripes, under-hood insulation, special nylon red stripe tires, 14x6 wheels, suspension features, fender "SS" emblems and "SS" emblems on radiator grille and gas filler cap, and 325hp Turbo-Jet 396ci engine $263.30

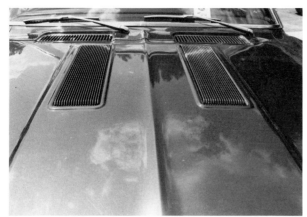

Small-block SS hood louvers for 1967-68 Camaro.

L78

Camaro SS: Includes special hood and ornaments, front header panel paint stripes, under-hood insulation, special nylon red stripe tires, 14x6 wheels, suspension features, fender "SS" emblems and "SS" emblems on radiator grille and gas filler cap, and 375hp Turbo-Jet 396ci engine $500.30

Z28

Special Performance Package: includes 320ci V-8 engine, closed positive ventilation, dual exhaust with deep tone mufflers, special front and rear suspension, heavy-duty radiator and temperature-controlled fan, quick ratio steering, 15x6 wheels, 7.35x15 nylon red stripe tires, 3.73:1 rear axle ratio, special paint stripes on hood and rear deck. Requires four-speed close ratio transmission, power brakes, front disc brakes, or heavy-duty front disc brakes with metallic rear brakes, posi-traction recommended. Available on Sport Coupe only $358.10

Special Performance Package Z281 includes above plus plenum air intake with special air cleaner and ducting system (furnished loose) $437.10

.Special Performance Package Z282 includes basic special performance package with exhaust headers, furnished loose $779.40

.Special Performance Package Z283 includes basic special performance package with plenum air intake and exhaust headers, furnished loose $858.40

Power Teams

Engines:

L22	155hp Turbo-Thrift 250 six-cylinder	26.35
L30	275hp Turbo-Fire 327 V-8	92.70
	295hp Turbo-Fire 350 V-8 (see SS 350 option)	

Transmissions:

M13	Special fully-synchronized three-speed	79.00
M20	Four-speed wide range for six-cylinder models	184.35
M20	Four-speed wide range for eight-cylinder models	184.35
M21	Four-speed close ratio (302ci or 375hp 396ci engine required)	184.35
M35	Powerglide for six-cylinder models	184.35
M35	Powerglide for eight-cylinder models	194.85
M40	Turbo Hydra-matic (325hp engine req.)	226.45
G80	Posi-traction rear axle	42.15

Axle Ratios:

	Economy	2.15
	Performance	2.15
	Special	2.15
G94	Axle, 3.31:1 ratio	2.15
G96	Axle, 3.55:1 ratio	2.15
G97	Axle, 2.73:1 ratio	2.15
H01	Axle, 3.07:1 ratio	2.15
H02	Axle, 3.73:1 ratio	2.15

Power Assists

J50	Vacuum-power brakes	42.15
J56	Heavy-duty front disc brakes with metallic rear brakes (Z28 pkg. req.)	79.00
N40	Power steering	84.30
A31	Power windows	100.10

Exterior Features

U73	Manual rear antenna, not available with AM/FM radio	9.50
V31	Front bumper guards	12.65
V32	Rear bumper guards	9.50
B93	Door edge guards	3.20
D33	Mirror: left-hand outside remote-control	9.50
	Exterior Paint, solid colors	N.C.

Vinyl Roof Cover, Sport Coupe only

C08	Black	73.75
C08	Beige	73.75

Convertible Top, Manual:

C05	White	N.C.

C05   Black   N.C.
C05   Blue   N.C.
Convertible Top, Power:
C05/C06 White   52.70
C05/C06 Black   52.70
C05/C06 Blue   52.70
D91   Front End Accent Band, included when 295hp, 325hp, or 375hp engine is ordered   14.75
PQ2   Tires, 7.35x14 two-ply nylon white stripe (no charge with SS models)   52.00
PW6   Tires, D70x14 two-ply nylon red stripe (standard with SS models)   62.50
P58   Tires, 7.35x14 two-ply whitewall, original equipment   31.35
P01   Wheel Covers, four bright metal. Not available when disc brakes ordered   21.10
P02   Wheel Covers, four simulated wire. Not available when disc brakes order   73.75
N96   Wheel Covers, four mag-style. Not available when disc brakes are ordered   73.75

Interior Features

C60   Air Conditioning: Includes 61-amp Delcotron, heavy-duty radiator, and temperature-controlled radiator fan. Power steering recommended   356.00
AL4   Strato-back Seat, front (not available with convertible or center console)   26.35
A67   Folding Rear Seat   31.60
A39   Seat Belts: custom deluxe front and rear   6.35
Belts: Front Shoulder (driver and passenger)
AS1   Standard Type - for use with standard seat belts   23.20
A85   Custom Deluxe - available only when custom deluxe seat belts or appearance guard group is ordered   26.35
U35   Clock, Electric: Floor mounted (Included when special instrumentation is ordered. Not available when stereo tape system is ordered)   15.80
D55   Console: includes floor-mounted shift lever, compartment, and ashtray. Not available on SS 350 with standard transmission or Strato-back seat   47.40
M11   Floor Mounted Shift Lever (three-speed transmission and six-cylinder or 327ci engine required, included when center console ordered)   10.55
C50   Rear Window Defroster: Sport Coupe models only   21.10

Glass, Soft Ray Tinted:
A01   All windows   30.55

A02   Windshield only   21.10
AS2   Headrests, Strato-Ease: Driver and pass   52.70
U17   Instrumentation, Special: eight-cylinder models only. Available only when console is ordered. Includes ammeter, temperature, oil pressure, fuel gauges, and electric clock mounted on console; fuel level indicator light and tachometer mounted in instrument panel cluster   79.00

Lights:
U28   Ashtray   1.60
U29   Courtesy, Sport Coupe models only 4.25
U27   Glove compartment: included when Deluxe Interior Package is ordered   2.65
U25   Luggage   2.65
U26   Under-hood   2.65
B37   Mats, Floor: Color-keyed; (two) front and (two) rear   10.55
       Radios: Includes front antenna. Rear antenna must be ordered separately (see Exterior Features)   57.40
U63   Pushbutton control   57.40
U63/U80 Pushbutton control and rear seat speaker   70.60
U69   AM/FM pushbutton control   133.80
U69/U80 AM/FM pushbutton control and rear seat speaker   147.00
U57   Stereo Tape System, mounted below heater, includes four speakers (not available with air conditioning, Special Instrumentation, or radio with rear speaker)   128.50
U80   Rear Seat Speaker: For use with foundation group   13.20
U15   Speed Warning Indicator   10.55
K30   Speed and Cruise Control: (Cruise-Master) V-8 engines only. Available only when Powerglide transmission is ordered   50.05
N33   Steering Wheel, Comfortilt: Available only when optional transmission or console is ordered   42.15
N34   Steering Wheel, Sport-Styled, walnut-grained plastic ring   31.60
       Steering Wheel, Deluxe
N30   With custom interior   4.25
N30   Without custom interior   7.40
U57   Stereo Tape System: Mounted below heater. Includes four speakers. Not available when air conditioning or radio with rear speaker is ordered   128.50

Heavy-Duty and other Equipment

T60 Heavy-Duty Battery 7.40

J52 Brakes, Front Disc: Not available when metallic brakes are ordered 79.00

J65 Brakes, Special Metallic Facing: Available only when SS350 option is ordered 36.90

N10 Exhaust System: Dual, available only with 327 engines 21.10

N61 Exhaust System: Dual, with 275hp or 210hp engine only 21.10

N61 Exhaust System: Dual, with 295hp engine only N.C.

K02 Fan, Temperature-Controlled: eight-cylinder models only. Included when air conditioning is ordered 15.80

K19 GM Air Injector Reactor: Approved by the State of California for vehicle registration. Available only when closed engine positive ventilation is ordered 44.75

Generator

K79 42-amp Delcotron. Not available when air conditioning is ordered 10.55

K76 61-amp Delcotron. Included when air conditioning is ordered 21.10

C48 Heater and Defroster Deletion, Credit of 31.65

U03 Tri-Volume Horn: Sport Coupe models only 13.70

V01 Radiator, Heavy-Duty: Included when air conditioning is ordered 10.55

N44 Steering, Special: Includes quick-response steering; requires power steering when air conditioning is ordered 15.80

F41 Suspension, Special Purpose Front and Rear: Includes special front and rear springs and matching shock absorbers 10.55

K24 Ventilation, Closed Engine Positive 5.25

P12 Wheels, (five) 14x6 JK. Not available with SS350 option 5.30

Feature Groups

Appearance Guard Group: includes the following items: front and rear floor mats, door edge guards, front and rear bumper guards, and custom deluxe seat belts 42.25

Auxiliary Lighting Group

Convertible with Custom interior includes under-hood light, ashtray light, and luggage compartment light 6.90

Convertible without Custom interior includes under-hood light, ashtray light, luggage compartment light, and glove compartment light 9.55

Sport Coupe with Custom interior includes courtesy lights, under-hood light, ashtray light, and luggage compartment light 11.15

Sport Coupe without Custom interior includes courtesy lights, under-hood light, ashtray light, luggage compartment light, and glove compartment light 13.80

Foundation Group includes pushbutton radio and electric clock 72.70

Operating Convenience Group includes left outside remote-control rearview mirror and rear window defroster (Sport Coupe only) 30.60

Deluxe door panel for 1967 Camaro.

Dealer-installed air conditioning.

1967 model column shift.

Dealer-Installed Custom Features and Accessories

Description	Part No.
Air Conditioning, Comfort-Car	
Six-cylinder	987016
327 cu-in V-8	987017
Air Conditioning Adapter	
For use with 987017 and GM A.I.R.	987097
Antennas, Manual	
Right front, AM/FM	986822
Right front, AM	986819
Right rear, AM	986825
Power Brakes	986825
Locking Gas Filler Cap	986970
Deck Lid Carrier	986914
Electric Clock	987035
Compass	987092
Rear Window Defroster	986906
Emergency Road Kit	986792
Fire Extinguisher, 2 3/4 lb. dry chemical	985592
Fire Extinguisher Recharge Kit	985593
Temperature-Controlled Fan	
Six-cylinder	986067
327 cu-in V-8	985355
Contour Rubber Floor Mats, Front	
Turquoise	986987
Black	986986
Gold	986989
Blue	986988
Red	986985

Description	Part No.
Contour Rubber Floor Mats, Rear	
Turquoise	986993
Black	986992
Gold	986995
Blue	986994
Red	986991
Front Bumper Guards	986806
Rear Bumper Guards	986805
Door Edge Guards	986875
Tri-Volume Horn	986966
Lights	
Ashtray	986958
Glove Compartment	986916
Luggage Compartment	986876
Under-hood	987028
Courtesy	986938
Litter Container, Instrument Panel Mounted	986670
Spare Wheel Lock	987048
Vanity Visor Mirror	987029
Ski Rack, requires deck lid carrier	987066
Radio	
Manual AM, front antenna	986834
Manual AM, rear antenna	986855
Pushbutton AM, front antenna	986848
Pushbutton AM, rear antenna	986820
Pushbutton AM/FM, front antenna	986821
Rear Seat Speaker, except convertible	986931
Speed Control, Cruise-Master with Powerglide	987060
Speed Control Adapter for use with 987060 and three- or four-speed transmission	987061
Hand Portable Spotlight	987112
Stereo Multiplex System	
Multiplex	986932
Front Speaker	987065
Rear Speakers (two)	986931
Convertible speaker housings (two)	987056
Stereo Switch for use when both Multiplex and Tape Systems installed	987072
Stereo Tape System	
Tape player	987071
Front Speaker	987065
Rear Speakers (two)	986931
Convertible speaker housings (two)	987056
Tachometer	987099
Tissue Dispenser	986965
Wheel Covers, set of four	986678
Wheel Covers, Mag-Style, set of four	986067
Wheel Covers, Simulated Wire, set of four	987100

1967 Camaro Trim Plate

```
04A (A)R(B)        J316***
ST67 1 (C) 12667 (D)      NOR (E) 105753 BDY (F)
TR 732-Z (G)      0 (H)-1(I)              PNT
W (J)   2MG 9K)   3SL (L)
```

Location A - Build Date
01 - January
02 - February
03 - March
04 - April
05 - May
06 - June
07 - July
08 - August
09 - September
10 - October
11 - November
12 - December
A - 1st week of month
B - 2nd week of month
C - 3rd week of month
D - 4th week of month
E - 5th week of month

Location B - Interior Color Code
(Norwood cars only)
R - Bright Blue
G - Gold
B - Blue
E - Black
D - Red
T - Turquoise
K - Parchment/Black
Y - Yellow

***Van Nuys cars had this code. It is believed to be an internal plant code for dating of production. Example: J316 would have been the 316th car built during the "J" period, which looks to be approximately the third week in April. It is believed that around 300 cars were produced during each letter designation. Examples: 04A - G238 and 04B - H433.

Location C - Model Year
1967

Location D - Interior Style Code
12437 - Sport Coupe, standard interior
12467 - Convertible, standard interior
12637 - Sport Coupe, custom interior
12667 - Convertible, custom interior

Location E - Assembly Plant
NOR - Norwood, Ohio
LOS - Van Nuys, California

Location F - Body Unit Number

Location G - Interior Trim
707 - Yellow custom buckets
709 - Gold standard buckets
711- Gold custom buckets
712 - Gold custom bench
716 - Bright blue custom bench
717 - Blue standard buckets
732 - Bright blue custom buckets
739 - Blue standard bench
741 - Red standard buckets
742 - Red custom buckets
756 - Black standard bench
760 - Black standard buckets
765 - Black custom buckets
767 - Black custom bench
779 - Turquoise custom buckets
796 - Gold standard bench
797 - Parchment custom buckets
Z - Custom bucket seat appointments
H - Bench seat
Y - Factory Headrests

Location H - Lower Body Color
AA - Tuxedo Black
CC - Ermine White
DD - Nantucket Blue
EE - Deepwater Blue
FF - Marina Blue
GG - Granada Gold
HH - Mountain Green
KK - Emerald Turquoise
LL - Tahoe Turquoise
MM - Royal Plum
NN - Madeira Maroon
RR - Bolero Red
SS - Sierra Fawn
TT - Capri Cream
YY - Butternut Yellow

Location I - Upper Body Color
Vinyl or Convertible top
    1 - White Top
    2 - Black top
Letters in this location (CC, etc.) from above chart indicate no vinyl top. CC - Ermine White lower and upper paint finish.

Protect-O-Plate from Los Angeles plant.

Location J - Option Information
Group 1

       W - tinted windshield

       E - all tinted windows

       X - power windows

       D - power convertible top

       L - fold-down rear seat

If Group 1 does not appear, none of the above options appeared on the car. This rule applies to all groupings.

Location K - Option Information
Group 2

       M - Powerglide transmission

       G - center console

       L - four-speed manual transmission

       E - air conditioning

       S - rear antenna

       B - three-speed on floor

       U - eight-track/multiplex

       R - rear seat speaker

Location L - Option Information
Group 3

       Interior/Exterior

       S - RPO Z23 option, interior decor

       L - Rally Sport Equipment

       K - RPO Z21 option, style trim group

       B - rear defogger

Location M - Option Information
Group 4

       4P - correct code for SS 350

       N - 396/325hp

       K - 396/375 L78

       L - 302 Z28

       F - remote mirror

If there was no designation in Group 4, the car was either a 327 V-8 or six-cylinder model.

Location N - Option Information
Group 5

       Y - deluxe seat belts

       Z - custom shoulder belts

       B - appearance group including bumper guards, floor mats, and door edge guards

1967 Camaro Protect-O-Plate

A Protect-O-Plate was furnished with all 1967 Camaros and was a metal plate imprinted at the assembly plant. The plate contained information on various standard or optional equipment. You may determine from the imprinted information on the plate the type of engine, transmission, rear axle, exterior color, the month the vehicle was produced, and other basic vehicle information.

G(A)	GG(B)	123677N123456(C)	H(D)
F0302MO(E)		QL0227G(F)	W(G)
P7B26(H)		1(I)1(J)4(K)3(L)4(M)5(N)1(O)	
			(P)
	Chevrolet Owner		
	124 Main St.		
	Anywhere, AB	3-15-67	
	USA		

Location A - 1967 Interior Colors
Note: All colors were not available on Camaro.

A - Red vinyl

B - Blue

C - Black vinyl

D - Red

E - Black

G - Gold

H - Blue vinyl

K - Parchment/Black

L - Black vinyl

N - Black cloth

R - Bright Blue

T - Turquoise

U - Blue vinyl (optional)

Y - Yellow

The colors listed below were not standardly available on Camaros but could be special ordered.

F - Fawn

M - Maroon

P - Plum

S - Blue cloth

V - Fawn vinyl

W - Gold cloth

Location B - 1967 Exterior Colors

AA - Tuxedo Black
CC - Ermine White
DD - Nantucket Blue
EE - Deepwater Blue
FF - Marina Blue
GG - Granada Gold
HH - Mountain Green
KK - Emerald Turquoise
LL - Tahoe Turquoise
MM - Royal Plum
NN - Madiera Maroon
RR - Bolero Red
SS - Sierra Fawn
TT - Capri Cream
YY - Butternut Yellow

Location C - Vehicle Identification Number

12437 - Sport Coupe, V-8 engine
12467 - Convertible, V-8 engine
12337 - Sport Coupe, six-cylinder
12367 - Convertible, six-cylinder

7 - Year (1967)

N - Plant (Norwood)
L - Plant (Los Angeles)

123456 - Sequential Body Number

Location D - Carburetor Source

B - Bay City
C - Carter
H - Holley
R - Rochester

Location E - Engine Production Code

F - Flint
T - Tonawanda
S - Saginaw
R - Rochester
K - McKinnon Industries

1-12 Month Production Code:
1 - January
2 - February
3 - March
4 - April
5 - May
6 - June
7 - July
8 - August
9 - September
10 - October

Protect-O-Plate from Norwood plant.

Trim tag.

11 - November
12 - December

01-31 Day of Month

1967 Engine Codes
LA - 230/140 with Manual Transmission
LB - 230/140 with Manual Transmission and CAC
LC - 230/140 with A.I.R.
LD - 230/140, Manual Transmission with A.I.R. and CAC
LE - 230/140 with Powerglide
LF - 230/140 with Powerglide and CAC
LG - 230/140 with Powerglide and A.I.R.
LH - 230/140 with Powerglide, A.I.R., and CAC
LN - 250/155 with Manual Transmission
LO - 250/155 with Manual Transmission and CAC
LP - 250/155 with Powerglide and A.I.R.
LQ - 250/155 Manual Transmission with A.I.R. and CAC
FM - 250/155 with Powerglide
FR - 250/155 with PG and CAC
GP - 250/155 with Powerglide and A.I.R.
GQ - 250/155 with PG, A.I.R., and CAC
MD - 283/195 two-barrel with four-speed transmission (4/67)

MJ - 283/195 two-barrel with Powerglide (4/67)
MO - 302/290 four-barrel with four-speed transmission (Z28)
MP - 302/290 four-barrel with four-speed transmission and A.I.R. (Z28)
MA - 327/210 two-barrel with Manual Transmission
MB - 327/210 two-barrel Manual Transmission with A.I.R.
ME - 327/210 two-barrel with Powerglide
MF - 327/210 two-barrel with PG and A.I.R.
MK - 327/275 four-barrel with Manual Transmission
ML - 327/275 four-barrel Manual Transmission with A.I.R.

MM - 327/275 four-barrel with Powerglide
MN - 327/275 four-barrel with PG and A.I.R.
MS - 350/295 with Manual Transmission
MT - 350/295 Manual Transmission with A.I.R.
MU - 350/295 with Powerglide
MV - 350/295 with Powerglide and A.I.R.
EI - 396/325 HD Manual Transmission with A.I.R.
EQ - 396/325 L35 with Turbo Hydra-matic
EY - 396/325 L35 with A.I.R.
MQ - 396/375 L78
MR - 396/375 L78 with A.I.R.
MW - 396/325 L35
MX - 396/375 L78 with A.I.R.
MY - 396/375 L78 with Turbo Hydra-matic
MZ - 396 with three-speed auto and A.I.R.

Original sales literature.

Location F - Rear Axle Code
PA - 3.08
PB - 3.36
PC - 3.31
PD - 3.08 posi
PE - 3.08 posi
PF - 3.31 posi
PG - 3.36 posi
PH - 3.55
PI - 3.55
PJ - 3.73
PK - 3.55
PL - 3.55
PM - 3.07
PO - 3.07 posi
PP - 3.55
PQ - 3.55
PR - 3.31 posi
PS - 3.55 posi
PT - 3.73
PU - 3.73 posi
PV - 3.07

01-12 Month:
01 - January
02 - February
03 - March
04 - April
05 - May
06 - June
07 - July
08 - August
09 - September
10 - October
11 - November
12 - December

01-31 Day of Month

Plant Codes:
W - Warren
G - Chevrolet Gear and Axle
B - Buffalo
K - McKinnon

Location G - Month of Vehicle Build
V - August 1966
L - September 1966
R - October 1966
K - November 1966
Z - December 1966
S - January 1967
P - February 1967
W - March 1967

N - April 1967
Y - May 1967
T - June 1967
X - July 1967

Location H - Transmission Number
K - McKinnon Industries four-speed
C - Cleveland Powerglide
M - Muncie three-speed
R - Saginaw four-speed
T - Toledo Powerglide
K - McKinnon Industries three-speed
P - Muncie four-speed
E - McKinnon Industries Powerglide
H - Muncie Heavy-Duty
A - Cleveland Torque Drive
X - Cleveland THM 350
B - Cleveland THM 350
Y - Toledo THM 350
7 - Model Year (1967)
A-T Calendar Month:
A - January
B - February
C - March
D - April
E - May
H - June
K - July
M - August
P - September
R - October
S - November
T - December
01-31 Day of Month
Turbo Hydra-matic Code: Contains model year, model identification, and production date.
67 - Year 1967
Engine Identification:
A - 396ci
B - 427ci
C - 396ci (Chevelle/Camaro)
D - 327ci
Build Date: Code of 1967 model year begins with first day of the calendar year 1966 and continues through the 1967 calendar year.

Location I - Power Brakes/Power Steering
1 - N40 Power Steering only
2 - J50 Power Brakes only
3 - N40 and J50 Power Steering and Power Brakes

Location J - 1967 Radio/Clock Group
1 - Chevrolet, Chevelle, Chevy II, Corvair, and Camaro.

Location K - 1967 Radio Option
3 - U63 AM Radio
4 - U63/U80 AM Radio with rear speaker
5 - U69 AM/FM Radio
6 - U69/U80 AM/FM Radio with rear speaker

Location L - 1967 Disc Brake Option
3 - J52 Disc Brakes
5 - F41/J52 Special Suspension with Disc Brakes

Location M - Air Conditioning Option
1 - C60 Air Conditioning
4 - C48 Heater Delete

Location N - 1967 Power Window Equipment Option
1 - A31 Power Windows
5 - A31/B93 Power Windows and Door Edge Guards

Location O - Power Seat Equipment
Power seat equipment was not available on a Camaro.

Location P - Chevrolet Bow Tie Emblem

This 1967 Camaro sports a big block. The crossed-flags emblem on the fender indicate a 396 powerplant.

The bumblebee stripe on 1967 SS Camaro's broke at the SS emblem and continued to the bumper.

1967 Camaro rally wheels were a two-piece design. The ornament read "DISC BRAKE" if the car was so equipped.

Otherwise just CHEVROLET MOTOR DIVISION would appear.

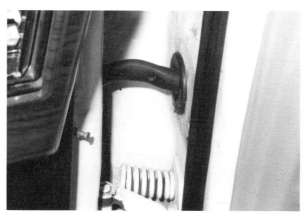

Power windows, available from 1967 to 1969, were discontinued in 1970 and did not reappear until late in the second generation. All power windowed Camaros had this boot to hold wiring from the dash to the door.

1967 Indy Pace Car showing rear antenna option.
Rear spoiler equipped cars were not allowed this option.

1967 Camaro with SS 350 option. The SS 350 horn button was the only reference to the SS option on the interior.

View the inner-workings of a Muncie 4-speed transmission
used on first generation Camaros.

Crossram with cowl-plenum set up was not factory-in-
stalled. These are very rare and were only installed on 1967
and 1968 Camaros.

Chapter 2

1968 Camaro

1968 Manufacturer's suggested retail price (MSRP) for base model Camaros

Model Number	Description	MSRP
12337	six-cylinder Sport Coupe	$2,565.00
12367	six-cylinder convertible	2,802.00
12437	eight-cylinder Sport Coupe	2,670.00
12467	eight-cylinder convertible	2,908.00

Note: Manufacturer's suggested retail price (**MSRP**) includes the factory delivery and handling charge (including federal excise tax) and recommended dealer delivery and handling charge. This price does not include transportation charges, state and local taxes, or any accessories or optional equipment that may be ordered.

Camaro Standard Equipment

Protective inner skirts at both front and rear wheel openings; flush-and-dry rocker panels; energy-absorbing steering column; seat belts with pushbutton buckles for all passenger positions; passenger-guard door locks with deflecting lock buttons on all doors; four-way hazard warning flasher; dual master cylinder brake system with warning light and corrosion-resistant brake lines; latches on folding seat backs; dual-speed windshield wipers and washers; outside rearview mirror; back-up lights; new side marker lights and parking lights that illuminate with headlights; padded instrument panel, sun visors, windshield pillars; reduced-glare instrument panel top, inside windshield moldings, horn button, steering wheel hub, and windshield wiper arms and blades; inside day-night mirror with deflecting base; lane change feature in direction signal control; safety armrests; thick-laminate windshield; soft, low-profile window control knobs and coat hooks; energy-absorbing seat backs; yielding door and window control handles; energy-absorbing instrument panel with smooth contoured knobs and levers; tire safety rim; safety door latches and hinges; uniform shift quadrant; energy-absorbing steering wheel; snag-resistant steering wheel hardware; fuel tank and filler pipe security; high-level ventilation system; built-in blended-air heater and defroster system; Magic-Mirror acrylic lacquer finish; friction-type ventipanes; curved solid tempered plate glass side and rear windows; two-key lock system; weather-shielded key locks; pushbutton-type outside door handles; Astro-Ventilation system with full door glass styling; color-keyed interior trim; scuff-resistant plastic cowl side panels with molded-in ventilator grilles; quality interior features and appointments; full-view instrument panel with instruments and controls; and locking glove compartment.

Consult authorized Chevrolet Dealers or your Fleet Representative for information on accessories and extra cost of optional equipment not listed.

General Motors Corporation reserves the right to make changes at any time, without notice, in prices, colors, materials, equipment, accessories, specifications, and models, and to discontinue models.

Serial Numbers and Identification
Vehicle Identification Number (VIN)

Six-cylinder example:

Model	Model Year (1968)	Assembly Plant (Los Angeles)	Unit Number (25th unit)
12237	8	L	300025

Therefore: The 25th model built at Los Angeles would be serial number 123378L300025.

Above and below, standard 1968 Camaro from front and rear.

Eight-cylinder example:

	Model Year	Assembly Plant	Unit Number
Model	(1968)	(Norwood)	(26th unit)
12437	8	N	300026

Therefore: The 26th model built at Norwood would be serial number 124378N300026.

Hood louvers found on 1968-69 Camaros.

Assembly Plants
L - Los Angeles
N - Norwood
Starting unit number was 300001 and up at each plant regardless of series.
Location: Stamped on plate attached to metal dash panel on driver's side.

Basic Specifications
Overall Length, in.	184.6
Overall Width, in.	72.3
Overall Height, in.	50.9
Wheelbase, in.	108.0
Front Tread, in.	59.6
Rear Tread, in.	59.5
Curb Weight, lbs.	2950
Usable Trunk Area, cu. ft.	8.3
Fuel Capacity, gal.	18

Standard six-cylinder in 1968 Camaro.

Transmission Identification

Example: QBS8E01D
QB - Type
QB - three-speed L6 and V-8
S - Saginaw
HI - four-speed L6
P - Muncie
R - Saginaw
XJ - four-speed V-8
P - Muncie
R - Saginaw
TB - Powerglide L6
C - Cleveland
T - Toledo
YH - Powerglide V-8
C - Cleveland
T - Toledo
- Turbo Hydra-Matic V-8
CC - Ypsilanti
Location:
Three- and four-speeds are stamped on the right-hand side of the case in upper front corner.
Four-speeds are stamped on top right side of case.
Powerglides are stamped on right side of pan.
Turbo Hydra-matics have a nameplate tag on right side of case.
Production Month Codes:
A - January
B - February
C - March
D - April
E - May
H - June
K - July
M - August
P - September
R - October
S - November
T - December
01 - 1st day of the month
D or N - Day or Night shift

Engine Identification

Example: F 1210 BA
F - Flint (source designation)
1210 - Production Month and Date
      12 - December
      10 - 10th day
BA - Type designation

Types:
230ci six-cylinder
BA - Regular production engine, three-speed
BF - Regular engine, Powerglide

250ci six-cylinder (RPO L22)
CM - Optional engine, three- or four-speed transmission
CQ - Optional engine, Powerglide

302ci eight-cylinder (RPO Z28)
MO - Special engine, manual transmission

327ci eight-cylinder
MA - Regular production, three- or four-speed, two-barrel carburetor
ME - Regular engine, Powerglide

327ci eight-cylinder (RPO L30)
MK - Optional engine, three- or four-speed, four-barrel carburetor
MM - Optional engine, Powerglide, four-barrel carburetor

350ci eight-cylinder(RPO L48)
MS - Optional engine, three- or four-speed, four-barrel carburetor
MU - Optional engine, Powerglide, four-barrel carburetor

396ci eight-cylinder (RPO L35)
MW - Optional engine, three- or four-speed, four-barrel carburetor
MY - Optional engine, Hydra-matic

Location:
Six-cylinder models are stamped on pad on right side of cylinder block to rear of distributor.
Eight-cylinder models are stamped on pad at front right side of cylinder block.

Rear Axle Identification
Example: PE 0212 B
PE - Type Designation
PE - 3.08, three- or four-speed and Powerglide
PX - 2.73, three-speed transmission
BK - 2.73, four-speed and Powerglide
QT - 2.73, Turbo Hydra-matic transmission
QJ - 3.07, three- or four-speed and Powerglide
QL - 3.31, three- or four-speed and Powerglide
0212 - Production Month and Date
      02 - February
      12 - 12th day
B - Source Designation
      B - Buffalo
      G - Gear & Axle Plant
      W - Warren
Stamping location is next to carrier housing.

1968 Camaro Regular Equipment—Exterior

Bright Trim and Ornamentation

Windshield reveal molding	all
Windshield pillar molding	convertible only
Front header panel nameplate	all
Radiator grill emblem	all
Body sill molding, slender	all
Front fender nameplate	all
Front fender engine emblem (V-8, and optional L6)	all
Hubcaps	all
Rear window reveal molding	coupe only
Rear belt molding	convertible only
Rear deck lid nameplate	all
Rear-quarter window glass channel, front	all

Other Exterior

Plastic radiator grille	all
Grille mounted parking lights	all
Fuel filler cap, in rear panel	all
Front and rear marker lamps	all

1968 Camaro Regular Equipment—Interior

Interior Bright Trim

Door and window control arms	all
Door sill plates	all
Rearview mirror, day-night padded frame	all
Rearview mirror support - deflecting	all
Seat adjuster handle	all
Sunshade supports	all

Instrument Panel

Ashtray	all
Astro-ventilation air outlets, bright	all
Cigarette lighter	all
Courtesy lamps	convertible only
Instrument cluster bezel	all
Instrument panel center trim plate - black texture	all
Temp, ammeter, oil pressure warning lights	all
Radio hole cover plate	all
Glove compartment door nameplate, "Camaro"	all

Other Interior

Front door padded armrest with bright molding	all
Rear quarter panel armrest and ashtray, built in	convertible only
Roof center dome light	coupe only
Front door jamb light switch	all
Steering wheel, three-spoke, horn button	all
Vent control knobs, trim color	all
Door lock buttons, trim color	all
Passenger compartment floor covering, carpet	all
Seats, front bucket	all
Padded windshield pillars	all

1968 Camaro Major Appearance and Performance Options

Custom interior RPO Z87)

Deluxe seat and sidewall trim
Door pull handle back plate
Additional body insulation
Molded trunk mat
Glovebox lamp
Under-hood insulation
Instrument panel peripheral molding
Bright pedal pads
Instrument panel assist handle
New deluxe steering wheel, horn blowing buttons and special hub emblem
Woodgrain instrument panel center trim plate (includes smooth black ashtray face plate)

Special Interior Group (RPO Z23)

Instrument panel peripheral molding
Bright pedal pads
New deluxe steering wheel, horn blowing buttons and special hub emblem
Woodgrain instrument panel center trim plate (includes smooth black ashtray face plate)

Rally Sport Package (RPO Z22)

(includes Style Trim Group RPO Z21)
Special radiator grille; concealed headlights
Parking lights in front valance
Special taillights
Back-up lights in rear valance
"RS" fuel filler cap, grille and front fender emblems
"RS" steering wheel hub emblem (standard wheel only)
Body side lower molding with black paint below
Belt reveal molding
Wheel opening moldings
Bright roof drip molding (coupe only)

Style Trim Group (RPO Z21)

(included in Rally Sport Package RPO Z22)
Belt reveal molding
Wheel opening moldings
Bright roof drip molding (coupe only)

Vinyl Roof (RPO C08)

Black or White - coupe only
Bright roof drip molding
Vinyl top material
Rear quarter and tulip panel molding

Optional console and gauges.

Standard door panel from 1968 model.

Standard door glass.

Camaro SS with 350 V-8 (RPO L48)

Under-hood insulation
Front header and body side paint stripes (revised January 1968)
Red stripe tires, wide oval F70-14-4PR
"SS" fuel filler cap, grille, and front fender emblems
"SS" steering wheel hub emblem (carried over for standard; new for deluxe wheel)
Special hood with simulated grilles
350ci V-8 engine; Bright engine chrome
Special front and rear leaf springs; finned front brake drums
Engine emblems on front fender (replaces standard V-8 emblem)

Camaro SS with 396 V-8 (RPO L34, L35, L78)

Under-hood insulation
Front header and body side paint stripes (revised January 1968)
Red stripe tires, wide oval F70-14-4PR
"SS" fuel filler cap, grille, and front fender emblems
"SS" steering wheel hub emblem (carried over for standard; new for deluxe wheel)
396ci V-8 engine
Black painted rear end panel
Special hood with simulated "air intakes"
Special front and rear shock absorbers
Special front and rear springs; finned front brake drums

Engine emblems on front fender (replaces standard V-8 emblem)
Bright engine chrome

302ci, Sport Coupe only (RPO Z28)

Bright engine chrome; 302ci V-8 engine
Hood and deck lid paint stripes
Red stripe tires, "NF" 7.35-15-4PR on 6" rims

RS & SS Options Combined

Under-hood insulation
Special radiator grille; Concealed headlights
Parking lights in front valance
Special taillights

Back-up lights in rear valance
Body side lower molding with black paint below
Belt reveal molding
Wheel opening moldings
Bright roof drip molding (coupe only)
Front header and body side paint stripes (revised January 1968)
Red stripe tires, wide oval F70-14-4PR
"SS" fuel filler cap, grill, and front fender emblems
"SS" steering wheel hub emblem (carried over for standard; new for deluxe wheel)
Special hood with simulated grilles (RPO L48 only)
350ci V-8 engine (RPO L48 only)
396ci V-8 engine (RPO L34, L35, L78 only)
Black painted rear end panel (RPO L34, L35, L78 only)
Special hood with simulated "air intakes" (RPO L34, L35, L78 only)
Special front and rear shock absorbers (RPO L34, L35, L78 only)
Special front and rear springs
Finned front brake drums
Engine emblems on front fender (replaces standard V-8 emblem)
Bright engine chrome

Striping on 1968 SS.

Special wide chrome on 1968 Camaro.

1968 Camaro Major Appearance and Performance Options: Interior Features and Appointments
Custom interior (RPO Z87)
Deluxe steering wheel with horn tabs
Bright outline molding around instrument panel
Special woodgrain accents
Black textured-finish trim plate with bright molding
Astro-Ventilation system with ball-type adjustable air outlets
Bright instrument bezels
Oil pressure, temperature, and generator warning lights
Parking brake and brake system warning light
Color-keyed turn signal and shift lever knobs
Bright control knobs
Padded instrument panel
Cigarette lighter
Electric clock (optional)
Glove compartment door nameplate
Glove compartment lock
Glove compartment light
Passenger assist grip
Molded vinyl door trim with integral armrest and carpeted lower panel

Interior of 1968 SS equipped with air conditioning.

Pull-type door opening handles
Scuff-resistant plastic cowl side panels
Bright window regulator handles with color-keyed knobs
Front door armrests
Rear armrests with built-in ashtrays (standard on convertible only)
Strato-bucket front seats
Fold-down rear seat back (optional)
All-vinyl seat trim (special fabric available for bucket seat Sport Coupe)
Foam-cushioned front seat
Folding front seat back latches
Shoulder belts - front (except convertibles)
Seat belts - front and rear with pushbutton buckles
Front seat belt retractors
Embossed vinyl headlining (Sport Coupe only)
Padded sun visors with center support
Color-keyed deep-twist floor carpeting
Day-night rearview mirror with vinyl edge
Padded windshield pillars
Bright foot pedal trim
Color-keyed coat hooks (Sport Coupe only)
Molded luggage compartment mat
Spatter-painted luggage compartment
Four-way hazard warning flasher switch on steering column
Interior light switch (in headlight switch)
Automatic front door courtesy/dome light switches
Center dome light (Sport Coupe only)
Dual instrument panel courtesy lights (standard on convertible only)
Convertible power-operated folding top (optional)

Special Interior Group (RPO Z23)
Deluxe steering wheel with horn tabs
Special woodgrain accents
Black-textured finish trim plate with bright molding
Astro-Ventilation system with ball-type adjustable air outlets
Bright instrument bezels
Oil pressure, temperature, and generator warning lights
Parking brake and brake system warning light
Color-keyed turn signal and shift lever knobs
Bright control knobs
Padded instrument panel
Cigarette lighter
Electric clock (optional)
Glove compartment door nameplate
Glove compartment lock
Glove compartment light (optional)
Passenger assist grip
Vinyl door and sidewall trim panels

Scuff-resistant plastic cowl side panels
Bright window regulator handles with color-keyed knobs
Front door armrests
Rear armrests with built-in ashtrays (standard on convertible only)
Strato-bucket front seats
Fold-down rear seat back (optional)
All-vinyl seat trim (special fabric trim available for bucket seat Sport Coupe)
Foam-cushioned front seat
Folding front seat back latches
Shoulder belts - front (except convertibles)
Seat belts - front and rear with pushbutton buckles
Front seat belt retractors
Embossed vinyl headlining (Sport Coupe only)
Padded sun visors with center support
Color-keyed deep-twist floor carpeting
Day-night rearview mirror with vinyl edge
Padded windshield pillars
Bright foot pedal trim
Color-keyed coat hooks (Sport Coupe)
Spatter-painted luggage compartment
Four-way hazard warning flasher switch on steering column
Interior light switch (in headlight switch)
Automatic front door courtesy/dome light switches
Center dome light (Sport Coupe only)
Dual instrument panel courtesy lights (standard on convertible only)
Convertible power-operated folding top (optional)

Standard Interior
Deluxe steering wheel with horn tabs (optional)
Steering wheel with horn button
Black textured-finish trim plate with bright molding
Astro-Ventilation system with ball-type adjustable air outlets
Bright instrument bezels
Oil pressure, temperature, and generator warning lights
Parking brake and brake system warning light
Color-keyed turn signal and shift lever knobs
Bright control knobs
Padded instrument panel
Cigarette lighter
Electric clock (optional)
Glove compartment door nameplate
Glove compartment lock
Glove compartment light (optional)
Vinyl door and sidewall trim panels
Scuff-resistant plastic cowl side panels
Bright window regulator handles with color-keyed knobs

Front door armrests
Rear armrests with built-in ashtrays (standard on convertible only)
Strato-bucket front seats
Fold-down rear seat back (optional)
All-vinyl seat trim (special fabric trim available for bucket seat Sport Coupe)
Foam-cushioned front seat
Folding front seat back latches
Shoulder belts - front (except convertibles)
Seat belts - front and rear with pushbutton buckles
Front seat belt retractors
Embossed vinyl headlining (Sport Coupe only)
Padded sun visors with center support
Color-keyed deep-twist floor carpeting
Day-night rearview mirror with vinyl edge
Padded windshield pillars
Color-keyed coat hooks (Sport Coupe)
Spatter-painted luggage compartment
Four-way hazard warning flasher switch on steering column
Interior light switch (in headlight switch)
Automatic front door courtesy/dome light switches
Center dome light (Sport Coupe only)
Dual instrument panel courtesy lights (standard on convertible only)
Convertible power-operated folding top (optional)

1968 Camaro Exterior Features and Identification
Camaro SS (RPO L48 or L35)
Front hood panel nameplate
"RS" or "SS" grille emblems
Rectangular parking/turn signal lights in grille
Color-keyed front accent band
Special domed hood with simulated air intakes
Windshield reveal molding
Camaro front fender nameplates
"SS" front fender emblems
Full door glass styling without ventipanes
Rectangular outside rearview mirror
Body side striping available at extra cost
Side marker lights, front and rear
Special SS wheels
Red stripe wide-oval tires (white stripe optional)
Rear window reveal molding (Sport Coupe only)
Deck lid nameplate
Black-finished rear body panel with accent stripe (with optional 396 only; except with Tuxedo Black exterior)
"RS" or "SS" fuel filler cap emblems
Single unit taillights with built-in back-up lights

Rally Sport (RPO Z22)
Front hood panel nameplate
Special full-width grille with concealed headlights
"RS" or "SS" grille emblems
Parking/turn signal lights mounted below front bumper
Color-keyed front accent band (available at extra cost)
Windshield reveal molding
Bright front and rear wheel opening moldings
Rally Sport front fender nameplates
Bright roof drip moldings (Sport Coupe only)
Full door glass styling without ventipanes
Rectangular outside rearview mirror
Bright belt moldings
Body side striping (available at extra cost)
Bright lower body side moldings
Black-finished lower body (except some exterior colors)
Side marker lights, front and rear
Hubcaps
Wheel covers (available at extra cost)
Rear window reveal molding (Sport Coupe only)
Deck lid nameplate
"RS" or "SS" fuel filler cap emblems
Dual-unit taillights
Back-up lights mounted below rear bumper

Style Trim Group (RPO Z21)
Front hood panel nameplate
Rectangular parking/turn signal lights in grille
Color-keyed front accent band (available at extra cost)
Windshield reveal molding
Bright front and rear wheel opening moldings
Camaro front fender nameplates
Bright roof drip moldings (Sport Coupe only)
Full door glass styling without ventipanes
Rectangular outside rearview mirror
Bright belt moldings
Body side striping (available at extra cost)
Body sill moldings
Side marker lights, front and rear
Hubcaps
Wheel covers (available at extra cost)
Rear window reveal molding (Sport Coupe only)
Deck lid nameplate
Single-unit taillights with built-in back-up lights

Standard Camaro
Front hood panel nameplate
Rectangular parking/turn signal lights in grille
Color-keyed front accent band (available at extra cost)

Front end of standard 1968 SS.

FBase coupe, 1967.

Windshield reveal molding
Camaro front fender nameplates
Full door glass styling without ventipanes
Rectangular outside rearview mirror
Body side striping (available at extra cost)
Body sill moldings
Side marker lights, front and rear
Hubcaps
Wheel covers (available at extra cost)
Rear window reveal molding (Sport Coupe only)
Deck lid nameplate
Single-unit taillights with built-in back-up lights

1968 Camaro Options and Accessories
When Factory Installed
V-8 Models (210hp Turbo-Fire 327 V-8)

12437	Sport Coupe	$2,670.00
12467	Convertible	2,908.00

Six-cylinder Models (140hp Turbo-Thrift 230 Six)

12337	Sport Coupe	2,565.00
12367	Convertible	2,802.00

Option No.	Description	List Price

Camaro SS: Includes special hood, black accented grille and ornaments, front accent band, hood insulation, special red stripe tires, special suspension, bright engine accents, SS emblems on fenders, grille, and fuel filler cap.

L48	295hp Turbo-Fire 350 engine	$210.65
L35	325hp Turbo-Jet 396 engine	263.30
L34	350hp Turbo-Jet 396 engine	368.65
L78	375hp Turbo-Jet 396 engine	495.30
L89	375hp Turbo-Jet 396 engine with aluminum heads	868.95

Z87
Custom interior: Includes special seat and sidewall trim with molded front door armrests, deluxe steering wheel, wood-grained instrument panel trim and molding, glove compartment light, bright pedal pads, instrument panel assist handle and luggage compartment mat $110.60

Z23
Special Interior: Included with Custom interior. Includes bright pedal pads, deluxe steering wheel, and wood-grained instrument panel trim and molding $17.95

Z22
Rally Sport: Includes special grille with vacuum-operated headlight covers, front valance-mounted parking lights, lower body side moldings, belt reveal molding, wheel opening moldings, rear valance-mounted back-up lights, "RS" emblems on grille, fenders, and fuel filler cap. Sport Coupe also includes bright roof drip molding $105.35

Style Trim: Included with Rally Sport. Includes belt reveal molding, front and rear wheel opening moldings.

Z21   Convertible $31.60

Z21   Sport Coupe: also includes bright roof drip molding $42.15

Z281
Special Performance Package: Model 12437 only. Includes 302-cu in V-8 engine, dual exhaust with deep-tone mufflers, special front and rear suspension, heavy-duty radiator and temperature-controlled fan, quick ratio steering, 15x6 wheels, E70x15 special nylon red stripe tires, 3.73:1 ratio axle and special paint stripes on hood and rear deck. Available only when four-speed close ratio transmission, power brakes, front disc brakes, or heavy-duty front disc brakes with metallic rear brakes are ordered. Posi-traction rear axle recommended $400.25

Z282
Special Performance Package plus Plenum Air Intake: Includes special air cleaner and duct system, furnished loose $479.25

Z283
Special Performance Package plus Exhaust Headers: Includes special tuned exhaust headers, furnished loose $779.40

Z284
Special Performance Package plus Plenum Air Intake and Exhaust Headers: furnished loose$858.40

Feature Groups
Appearance Guard Group includes:

V31	A - Front Bumper Guards	12.65
V32	B - Rear Bumper Guards	12.65
B93	C - Door Edge Guards	4.25
B37	D - Color-keyed Floor Mats, two front, two rear	10.55

GRP1 For all models without special rear springs, includes A, B, C, D 40.10

GRP1 For all models with special rear springs, includes A, C, D 27.45

Operating Convenience Groups includes:

U35 A - Electric Clock: included when special instrumentation is ordered 15.80

D33 B - left-hand Outside Remote-Control Rearview Mirror 9.50

C50 C - Rear Window Defroster (Sport Coupe only) 21.10

GRP4 For Sport Coupe with special instrumentation, includes B, C 30.60

GRP4 For Sport Coupe without special instrumentation, includes A, B, C 46.40

GRP4 For Convertible with special instrumentation, includes B 9.50

GRP4 For Convertible without special instrumentation, includes A, B 25.30

Power Teams

Engines: See Power Team chart for complete engine specifications, model, and transmission availability.

L22 155hp Turbo-Thrift 250 six-cylinder 26.35
L30 275hp Turbo-Fire 327 V-8 92.70

Transmissions: See Power Team chart for availability

MB1 Torque-Drive: six-cylinder only, not available when center console, posi-traction, optional rear axle ratio, and floor shift transmission are ordered 68.65
M35 Powerglide, six-cylinder models 184.35
M35 Powerglide, V-8 models 194.85
M40 Turbo Hydra-matic 237.00
M13 Special three-speed 79.00
M20 Four-speed wide-range 184.35
M21 Four-speed close ratio 184.35
M22 Heavy-duty four-speed close ratio 310.70
G80 Axle, Posi-traction Rear 42.15

Axle Ratios: See Power Team chart for available combinations

AXL1 Economy 2.15
AXL2 Performance 2.15
Special (if axle ratio other than standard, economy or performance is desired; refer to Power Team chart for availability—then list ratio on order form in box under "Special Ratio") 2.15

Power Assists

J50-Power Brakes, with drum-type brakes 42.15
J50/J52 Power Brakes, with disc-type front brakes 100.10
N40 Power Steering 84.30
C06 Power Top: convertible models only 52.70
A31 Electric Windows 100.10

Other Options

C60 Air Conditioning, Four Season: Not available when 375hp or 302-cu in engine is ordered. Includes 61-amp Delcotron, heavy-duty radiator and temperature-controlled radiator fan. Power steering recommended 360.20

D80 Auxiliary Panel and Valance: (Spoiler) 32.65

D91 Band, Front End Accent: Not available when Camaro SS or Special Performance Package is ordered 14.75

T60 Battery, Heavy-Duty 7.40

Belts, Seat and Shoulder: In addition to or replacing standard belts

Standard Style Shoulder Belts
AS1 two front 23.20
AS1/AS5 Two front and two rear 46.40

Custom Deluxe Front and Rear Seat Belts
A39 With bucket front seats 7.90
A39 With optional Strato-back front seat 9.50

Custom Deluxe Shoulder Belts (requires Option A39)
A85 Two front 26.35
A85/AS4 Two front and two rear 52.70
ZK3 Bucket seats - five seat and two shoulder 11.10
ZK3 Strato-back seats - six seat and two shoulder 12.65

D55 Console: Includes floor-mounted shift lever, compartment, and ashtray. Not available on 295hp engine with standard transmission 50.60

N10 Dual Exhaust System: with 210hp or 275hp engine only 27.40

NF2 Dual Exhaust System: with 210hp or 275hp engines and deep-tone mufflers 27.40

NF2 Dual Exhaust System: with 295hp, 350hp, or 375hp engines only with deep-tone mufflers N.C.

K02 Temperature-Controlled Fan: V-8 models only, included when air conditioning or Special Performance Package is ordered 15.80

K79 Generator: 42-amp Delcotron, not available when air conditioning or Turbo Hydra-matic is ordered 10.55

K76   Generator: 61-amp Delcotron, with air conditioning   5.30

K76   Generator: 61-amp Delcotron, without air conditioning   26.35

A01   Glass, Soft Ray Tinted: all windows 30.55

A02   Glass, Soft Ray Tinted: windshield only   21.10

AS2   Head Restraints, Driver and Passenger   52.70

U03   Tri-Volume Horn   13.70

U17   Special Instrumentation: V-8 models with console only, includes ammeter, temperature, oil pressure, and fuel gauges mounted on console; electric clock and tachometer mounted in instrument panel cluster   94.80

U46   Light Monitoring System   26.35

Lighting, Auxiliary

A - Ashtray light

B - Courtesy lights

C - Glove compartment light

D - Luggage compartment light

E - Under-hood light

ZJ9   For Sport Coupe with Custom interior, includes A, B, D, E   11.10

ZJ9   For Sport Coupe without Custom interior, includes A, B, C, D, E   13.70

ZJ9   For Convertible with Custom interior, includes A, D, E   6.85

ZJ9   For Convertible without Custom interior, includes A, C, D, E   9.50

Paint, Exterior: Solid Colors   N.C.

V01   Radiator, Heavy-Duty: Included when air conditioning is ordered. Not available when 302-cu in or 396-cu in engine is ordered   13.70

Radio Equipment

U63   AM Radio, pushbutton with front antenna   61.10

U69   AM/FM Radio, pushbutton with front antenna   133.80

U69/U79 AM/FM Stereo Radio, pushbutton with front antenna   239.15

U73   Antenna, Manual Rear - not available with AM/FM radio or auxiliary panel and valance equipment   9.50

U80   Speaker, Rear Seat - not available when stereo is ordered   13.20

C082   Roof Cover, Vinyl: Black - Sport Coupe only   73.75

C081   Roof Cover, Vinyl: White - Sport Coupe only   73.75

A67   Folding Rear Seat   42.15

AL4   Strato-Back Front Seat. Sport Coupe models only. Not available when center console is ordered   32.65

M11   Floor-Mounted Shift Lever: Available only with standard three-speed transmission with six-cylinder or 327 V-8 engines or Turbo Hydramatic transmission. Included when center console is ordered   10.55

U15   Speed Warning Indicator   10.55

K30   Speed and Cruise Control: (Cruise-Master) V-8 models only. Available only when Powerglide transmission is ordered   52.70

G31   Special Rear Springs: Includes rear bumper guards   20.05

N44   Special Steering: Includes quick-response steering; requires power steering when air conditioning or 396-cu in engine is ordered   15.80

N33   Comfortilt Steering Wheel: Available only when automatic or floor-mounted transmission is ordered   42.15

N34   Sports-Styled Steering Wheel: Woodgrained plastic rim   31.60

N30   Deluxe Steering Wheel: Included when custom or special interior is ordered   4.25

U57   Stereo Tape System: Includes 4 speakers; console required when air conditioning is ordered   133.80

D90   Sport Striping: Included with Camaro SS   25.30

D91   Front Accent Band: not available with Camaro SS   14.75

D96   Accent Striping   13.70

F41   Suspension, Special Purpose Front and Rear: V-8 models only. Not available when Special Performance Package is ordered. Includes special front and rear springs and matching shock absorbers   10.55

C051   Convertible Top, Manual: White   N.C.

C052   Convertible Top, Manual: Black   N.C.

C054   Convertible Top, Manual: Blue   N.C.

KD5   Ventilation, HD Closed Engine Positive 6.35

N65   Space Saver Tire: Spare to replace 7.35x14 blackwall ($13.10 to replace 7.35x14 whitewall; $6.00 to replace F70x14 red or white stripe)   19.35

PW7   Tires: F70x14, two-ply white stripe (no charge with SS models)   64.75

PW8   Tires: F70x14, two-ply red stripe (no charge with SS models)   64.75

PY4   Tires: F70x14, two-ply belted white stripe ($26.55 with SS models)   26.55

P58   Tires: 7.35x14, two-ply whitewall, original equipment   31.35

P01   Wheel Covers, Bright Metal: not available with Z28   21.10

N95   Wheel Covers, Simulated Wire: not available with Z28   73.75

N96   Wheel Covers, Mag-Style: not available with Z28   73.75

PA2   Wheel Covers, Mag-Spoke: not available with Z28   73.75

ZJ7   Wheels, Rally: Available only when power disc brakes are ordered. Includes special wheel, hubcap and trim ring. Not available when Special Performance Package is ordered   31.60

Dealer-Installed Custom Features and Accessories

Description	Part No.
Air Conditioning, Comfort-Car requires adapter with all engines	987155
six-cylinder	987162
327 and 350 engines	987163
396 engine	987229
Air Conditioning Adapter	
Power steering with six-cylinder and Powerglide or three-speed	987405
396 engine with Turbo Hydra-matic	987424
Antennas, Manual	
Right Front	987182
Right Rear	987183
Power Brakes	987452
Locking Gas Filler Cap	986970
Deck Lid Carrier	987254
Electric Clock, console mounted	987185
Compass	987457
Rear Window Defroster, coupe only	987244
Emergency Road Kit	986792
Fire Extinguisher, 2 3/4 lb. dry chemical	985592
Fire Extinguisher Recharge Kit	985593
Temperature-Controlled Fan	
six-cylinder and 396-cu in engines	986067
V-8 except 396-cu in engine	985355
Front Bumper Guards	986806
Rear Bumper Guards	986805
Door Edge Guards	987268
Tri-Volume Horn	987400
Light Monitoring System	
Coupe	987443
Convertible	987444
Lights	
Ashtray	987281
Glove Compartment	987188
Luggage Compartment	987242
Under-hood	987225
Courtesy	987256

Litter Container, Instrument Panel Mounted	986670
Litter Container, Saddle Type	
Black	986607
Blue	986602
Fawn	986603
Red	986608
Spare Wheel Lock	987048
Contour Rubber Floor Mats, Front	
Turquoise	987355
Black	987348
Gold	987349
Blue	987347
Red	987358
Contour Rubber Floor Mats, Rear	
Turquoise	987360
Black	987351
Gold	987352
Blue	987350
Red	987363
Mirror, Outside-Right Hand	987202
Vanity Visor Mirror	987255
Ski Rack	987196
Radio, Pushbutton AM, Front Antenna	987278
Radio, Pushbutton AM/FM, Front Antenna	987297
Front Speaker	987438
Rear Speaker	987302
Rear Speaker Housing, convertible	987280
Speed Control, Cruise-Master with Powerglide	987459
Hand Portable Spotlight	987112
Stereo Multiplex System	
Multiplex	987429
Front Speaker	987438
Rear Speakers (two)	987192
Convertible Speaker Housings (two)	987280
Bracket-used with air conditioning	987064
Stereo Tape System	
Tape Player, with console	987414
Tape Player, without console	987439
Front Speaker	987438
Rear Speakers (two)	987192
Convertible Speaker Housings (two)	987280
Tape Cartridge	987118
Tachometer	987099
Tissue Dispenser, Instrument Panel Mounted	987403
Wheel Covers, set of four	987288
Wheel Covers, Mag-style, set of four	987067
Wheel Covers, Simulated Wire, set of four	987100

Heater delete option, 1968.

Original GM 1968-69 Rally Sport headlight actuator.

Smog equipment and air conditioning did not leave much room on the passenger side of this 1968 Camaro.

1968 Camaro Trim Plate

```
┌─────────────────────────────────────────────┐
│ 12D (A)                      J13***           │
│ ST 68(B)   -12437(C)   NOR(D) 592953(E) BODY  │
│ TR 717(F)              D(G)2(H)  PAINT         │
└─────────────────────────────────────────────┘
```

Location A - Build Date
01 - January
02 - February
03 - March
04 - April
05 - May
06 - June
07 - July
08 - August
09 - September
10 - October
11 - November
12 - December
A - 1st week of month
B - 2nd week of month
C - 3rd week of month
D - 4th week of month
E - 5th week of month
*** Again this code will only appear on Van Nuys assembled cars. See 1967 trim plate information for an explanation.

Location B - Model Year
1968

Location C - Body Style
12337 - six-cylinder Sport Coupe
12367 - six-cylinder Convertible
12437 - eight-cylinder Sport Coupe
12467 - eight-cylinder Convertible

Location D - Assembly Plant
NOR - Norwood, Ohio
LOS - Van Nuys, California

Location E - Sequential Body Number

Location F - Interior Trim
711 - Ivory (white) custom buckets
721 - Gold custom buckets
712 - Black standard buckets
722 - Gold standard buckets
713 - Black standard bench
723 - Gold standard bench
714 - Black custom buckets
724 - Red standard buckets
715 - Black custom bench
725 - Red custom buckets
716 - Ivory Houndstooth buckets
726 - Turquoise custom buckets
717 - Blue standard buckets
727 - Turquoise custom bench
718 - Blue standard bench
730 - Parchment custom buckets
719 - Blue custom buckets
749 - Black Houndstooth buckets
720 - Blue custom bench

Location G - Body Paint Code
A - Tuxedo Black
C - Ermine White
D - Grotto Blue
E - Fathom Blue
F - Island Teal
G - Ash Gold
H - Grecian Green
J - Rallye Green
K - Tripoli Turquoise
L - Teal Blue
N - Cordovan Maroon
O - Corvette Bronze
P - Seafrost Green
R - Matador Red
T - Palomino Ivory
U - LeMans Blue
V - Sequoia Green
Y - Butternut Yellow
Z - British Green
— - Special Order

Location H - Top Color Code
1 - White convertible top
2 - Black vinyl or convertible top
4 - Blue convertible top
6 - White vinyl top

```
G(A)      GG(B)      123677N123456(C)      H(D)
F0302MO(E)           QL0227G(F)            W(G)
P7B26(H)             1(I)1(J)4(K)3(L)4(M)5(N)1(O)
                                           (P)
                     Chevrolet Owner
                     123 Main St.
                     Anywhere, AB          3-15-67
                     USA
```

What's missing from this photo? If you said the radio, right you are! This 1968 Camaro sports the radio delete plate.

1968 Camaro Protect-O-Plate

A Protect-O-Plate was furnished with all 1968 Camaros. This was a metal plate imprinted at the assembly plant and contained information on various standard or optional equipment. You may determine from the imprinted information on the plate the type of engine, transmission, rear axle, exterior color, the month the vehicle was produced, and other basic vehicle information.

Location A - 1968 Interior Colors

B - Blue (cloth and vinyl)
D - Red (cloth and vinyl)
E - Black (cloth and vinyl)
G - Gold (cloth and vinyl)
K - Parchment/Black
P - Gold vinyl (optional)
Q - Black and White vinyl (optional)
T - Turquoise (cloth and vinyl)
U - Blue vinyl (optional)

Location B - 1968 Exterior Colors

AA - Tuxedo Black
CC - Ermine White
DD - Grotto Blue
EE - Fathom Blue
FF - Island Teal
GG - Ash Gold
HH - Grecian Green
JJ - Rallye Green
KK - Tripoli Turquoise
LL - Teal Blue
NN - Cordovan Maroon
OO - Corvette Bronze
PP - Seafrost Green
RR - Matador Red
TT - Palomino Ivory
UU - LeMans Blue
VV - Sequoia Green
YY - Butternut Yellow
ZZ - British Green
— - Special Paint

Location C - Vehicle Identification Number

12437 - Sport Coupe, V-8 engine
12467 - Convertible, V-8 engine
12337 - Sport Coupe, six-cylinder
12367 - Convertible, six-cylinder
8 - Year (1968)
N - Plant
      N- Norwood
      L - Los Angeles
123456 - Sequential Body Number

Location D - Carburetor Source

B - Bay City
C - Carter
H - Holley
R - Rochester

Location E - Engine Production Code

F - Flint
T - Tonawanda
S - Saginaw
R - Rochester

Tower-style hose clamps were used on radiator hoses and heater hoses from 1968 on.

K - McKinnon Industries
1-12 Month Production Code:
1 - January
2 - February
3 - March
4 - April
5 - May
6 - June
7 - July
8 - August
9 - September
10 - October
11 - November
12 - December
01-31 Day of Month
1968 Engine Codes
BA - 230/140 Manual Transmission with A.I.R.
BD - 230/140 Manual Transmission with CAC and A.I.R.
BF - 230/140 with Powerglide
CM - 250/155 Manual Transmission with A.I.R.

CN - 250/155 Manual Transmission with CAC and A.I.R.
CQ - 250/155 with Powerglide
CR - 250/155 with Powerglide and CAC
MO - 302/270 with Manual Transmission
MA - 327/210 Manual Transmission with A.I.R.
ME - 327/210 with Powerglide
MS - 350/295 Manual Transmission
MU - 350/295 with Powerglide
MQ - 396/375 L78
MR - 396/350 with Turbo Hydra-matic
MT - 396/375 with Aluminum Heads
MW - 396/325 Manual Transmission with A.I.R.
MX - 396/350 Manual Transmission
MY - 396/325 with Turbo Hydra-matic

Location F - Rear Axle Code
PA - 3.08
PB - 3.36
PC - 3.31
PD - 3.08 posi

PE - 3.08 posi
PF - 3.31 posi
PG - 3.36 posi
PH - 3.55
PI - 3.55
PJ - 3.73
PK - 3.55
PL - 3.55
PM - 3.07
PO - 3.07 posi
PP - 3.55
PQ - 3.55
PR - 3.31 posi
PS - 3.55 posi
PT - 3.73
PU - 3.73 posi
PV - 3.07
01-12 Production Month Code:
01 - January
02 - February
03 - March
04 - April
05 - May
06 - June
07 - July
08 - August
09 - September
10 - October
11 - November
12 - December
01-31 Day of Month
Plant Codes:
W - Warren
G - Chevrolet Gear and Axle
B - Buffalo
K - McKinnon

Location G - Month of Vehicle Build
8 - August 1967
9 - September 1967
0 - October 1967
N - November 1967
D - December 1967
1 - January 1968
2 - February 1968
3 - March 1968
4 - April 1968
5 - May 1968
6 - June 1968
7 - July 1968

Location H - Transmission Number
D - Saginaw three-speed OD
K - McKinnon Industries four-speed

C - Cleveland Powerglide
M - Muncie three-speed
R - Saginaw four-speed
T - Toledo Powerglide
K - McKinnon Industries three-speed
P - Muncie four-speed
E - McKinnon Industries Powerglide
H - Muncie Heavy-Duty
A - Cleveland Torque Drive
X - Cleveland THM 350
B - Cleveland THM 350
Y - Toledo THM 350
8 - Model Year (1968)
A-T Calendar Month:
A - January
B - February
C - March
D - April
E - May
H - June
K - July
M - August
P - September
R - October
S - November
T - December
01-31 Day of Month
Turbo Hydra-matic Code: Contains model year, model identification, and production date
68 - Year 1968
Engine Identification:
A - 396ci
B - 427ci
C - 396ci (Chevelle/Camaro)
D - 327ci
Build Date: Code of 1967 model year begins with first day of the calendar year 1966 and continues through the 1967 calendar year. Code of 1968 model year begins with first day of calendar year 1967 and continues through 1968 calendar year.

Location I - Power Brakes/Power Steering
1 - N40 Power Steering only
2 - J50 Power Brakes only
3 - N40 and J50 Power Steering and Power Brakes

Location J
This location was not used on 1968 Camaros

Location K - 1968 Radio Option
4 - U63/U80 AM Radio with rear speaker
5 - U69 AM/FM Radio
6 - U69/U80 AM/FM Radio with rear speaker
7 - U69/U79 AM/FM Radio with stereo

Finned SS hood louvers were used on 1967 and 1968 small block SS cars. 1969 Camaros and 1968 big block SS cars had the smoke-stack style louver.

Location L - 1968 Disc Brake Option
3 - J52 Disc Brakes
5 - F41/J52 Special Suspension with Disc Brakes
6 - J56 Heavy-Duty Disc Brakes
8 - F41/J56 Special Suspension with Heavy-Duty Brakes
9 - J52/J56 Disc brake fronts with metallic rear brakes

Location M - Air Conditioning Option
1 - C60 Air Conditioning
4 - C48 Heater Delete

Location N - 1968 Power Window Equipment Option
1 - A31 Power Windows
5 - A31/N65 Power Windows and Space Saver Spare Tire

Location O - Power Seat Equipment
Power seat equipment was not available on a Camaro

Location P - Chevrolet Bow Tie Emblem

Good view of front end suspension on this early Camaro.

Chapter 3

1969 Camaro

1969 Manufacturer's suggested retail price (MSRP) for base model Camaros

Model Number	Description	MSRP
12337	six-cylinder Sport Coupe	$2,726.00
12367	six-cylinder convertible	2,940.00
12437	eight-cylinder Sport Coupe	2,621.00
12467	eight-cylinder convertible	2,835.00

Note: Manufacturer's suggested retail price (**MSRP**) includes the factory delivery and handling charge (including federal excise tax) and recommended dealer delivery and handling charge. This price does not include transportation charges, state and local taxes, or any accessories or optional equipment that may be ordered.

Camaro Standard Equipment

Protective inner skirts at both front and rear wheel openings; flush-and-dry rocker panels; energy-absorbing steering column; seat belts with pushbutton buckles for all passenger positions; passenger-guard door locks with deflecting lock buttons on all doors; four-way hazard warning flasher; dual master cylinder brake system with warning light and corrosion-resistant brake lines; latches on folding seat backs; dual-speed windshield wipers and washers; outside rearview mirror; back-up lights; new side marker lights and parking lights that illuminate with headlights; padded instrument panel, sun visors, and windshield pillars; reduced-glare instrument panel top, inside windshield moldings, horn button, steering wheel hub, and windshield wipers arms and blades; inside day-night mirror with deflecting base; lane change feature in direction signal control; safety armrests; thick-laminate windshield; soft, low-profile window control knobs and coat hooks; energy-absorbing seat backs; yielding door and window control handles; energy-absorbing instrument panel with smooth contoured knobs and levers; tire safety rim; safety door latches and hinges; uniform shift quadrant; energy-absorbing steering wheel; snag-resistant steering wheel hardware; fuel tank and filler pipe security; high-level ventilation system; built-in blended-air heater and rear windows; two-key lock system; weather-shielded key locks; pushbutton-type outside door handles; Astro-Ventilation system with full door glass styling; color-keyed interior trim; scuff-resistant plastic cowl side panels with molded-in ventilator grilles; quality interior features and appointments; full-view instrument panel with instruments and controls; and locking glove compartment.

Consult authorized Chevrolet Dealers or your Fleet Representative for information on accessories and extra cost of optional equipment not listed.

General Motors Corporation reserves the right to make changes at any time, without notice, in prices, colors, materials, equipment, accessories, specifications, and models, and to discontinue models.

Body Structure

Semi-integral construction with unitized all-welded steel body and bolt-on front end sheet metal. Chassis front frame section securely attached to body at four reinforced, rubber-cushioned mounting points. Combined units form an integrated structure of exceptional strength and rigidity. Design features include:

The 1969 Camaro SS.

Vinyl top on a 1967 base coupe.

Deluxe door panel found on 1968-69 Camaros.

Hood insulation from 1967-69 Camaros.

Rugged box-section design roof rails, channel-type windshield and rear window headers, and box-section door and roof pillars.

Heavy-gauge steel roof panel with single flanged channel lateral reinforcing box on Sport Coupe.

High-strength double-walled cowl unit welded to instrument panel, dash panel, and front pillars.

Deeply ribbed and contoured floor panel with under-body reinforcing cross-members.

Heavy-gauge steel box-section body sills; extra-heavy gauge on Convertible for added rigidity.

Flush-and-dry body rocker panels.

Double-paneled hood, door, and deck lid construction.

Fully counterbalanced hood and deck lid.

Front and rear inner fender panel construction for improved corrosion protection.

Structural components and body panels protected from corrosion by various primer coatings, zinc coatings, and anti-rust compounds. Selected structural members heavily zinc-coated before assembly. Selected exposed under-surfaces protected by spray-on undercoating.

Sound Insulation

Asphalt-impregnated felt blanket sidewall, roof, and deck lid insulation.

Heavy-fiber and fiber board mat dash panel insulation.

Fiber board rear bulkhead insulation.

Mastic sound deadener on floor and tunnel under rear seat.

Jute pad and asphalt-impregnated felt floor insulation plus carpeting.

Spray-on asphalt-impregnated fiber sound deadener on inside surface of door outer panels, wheel housings, and selected under-body areas.

Thick fiberglass hood insulation on Camaro SS and models equipped with Custom interior.

Weather Sealing

Flush-mounted adhesively bonded windshield and rear window installation for improved appearance and more positive sealing.

Molded vinyl door windlaces.

Rubber-fabric glass run channels and solid rubber window sill seals.

Double-sealing formed rubber weather seals.

Formed rubber deck lid seal.

Special body seam and joint sealing compounds.

Serial Numbers and Identification
Vehicle Identification Number (VIN)
Example: 123379L500025

12337 - Model
        12337 - six-cylinder Sport Coupe
        12367 - six-cylinder convertible
        12437 - eight-cylinder Sport Coupe
        12467 - eight-cylinder convertible
9 - Model Year (1969)
L - Assembly Plant
        L - Los Angeles
        N - Norwood
500025 - Unit Number

Locations: Upper right side of cowl panel on "firewall tag," right front fender under heater box, cylinder block, and transmission

Basic Specifications

Overall Length, in.	186.0
Overall Width, in.	74.0
Overall Height, in.	51.6
Wheelbase, in.	108.0
Front Tread, in.	59.6
Rear Tread, in.	59.5
Curb Weight, lbs.	3120

Usable Trunk Room, cu. ft.	8.5
Fuel Capacity, gal.	18

1969 Production Statistics

Total 1969 Camaros	243,095
SS Camaros	33,980
RS Camaros	37,773
Z/28 Camaros	20,302
Convertibles	17,573
Z10	NA
V-8	178,087
Six-cylinder	65,008
Indy Replicas	3,675
Indy Track Cars	2
JL8	206
L89	311
COPO	NA
ZL1	69

Time Built Code

This coding is for Norwood cars only. It is unknown whether Los Angeles cars used the same coding.

August 1968	N500001 - N502000
September 1968	N503000 - N512000
October 1968	N513000 - N535000
November 1968	N536000 - N554000
December 1968	N555000 - N570000
January 1969	N571000 - N591000
February 1969	N592000 - N614000
March 1969	N615000 - N627000
April 1969	N628000 - N635000
May 1969	N636000 - N654000
June 1969	N655000 - N664000
July 1969	N665000 - N670000
August 1969	N671000 - N678000
September 1969	N679000 - N694000
October 1969	N695000 - N710000
November 1969	N710000 - N711000

Notes: The 1969 Camaro had a long production year due to many reasons. The correlation between the time built code and VIN number could be plus or minus one production week. The 1970 1/2 Camaro was released in February 1970.

1969 Camaro Features—Interior

All vinyl bucket seat interior
Bright accents on instrument panel and doors
Foam-cushioned front and rear seats
Courtesy lights under instrument panel (convertible only)
Astro-Ventilation system with adjustable vent ports on instrument panel
Color-keyed deep-twist carpeting
Glove compartment lock
Cigarette lighter mounted in ashtray
Center dome light (except convertible)

Special Interior Group (RPO Z23)

Wood-grained accents on instrument panel and steering wheel
Assist grip and trim plate on instrument panel
Bright pedal trim

Custom interior (RPO Z87)

Choice of deluxe all-vinyl or luxurious hound's-tooth cloth and vinyl seats
Molded door panels with built-in armrest, door pulls, and carpeted lower panel
Wood-grained accents on instrument panel and steering wheel
Assist grip and trim plate on instrument panel
Bright pedal trim
Glove compartment light
Special body insulation
Luggage compartment mat

1969 Camaro Features—Exterior

Silver-finish grille
White lenses over amber parking/direction signal lights
Front fender engine emblems (except 140hp six-cylinder)
Front fender nameplates - "Camaro"
Windshield molding
Full door glass styling
Rectangular outside rearview mirror
Body sill molding
Hubcaps
Side marker lights - front and rear
Simulated rear fender louvers
Rear window molding (except convertible)
Triple-unit taillights with built-in back-up lights
Rear bumper guards
Concealed fuel filler

Style Trim Group (RPO Z21)

Fender striping
Simulated rear fender louvers with bright edges
Wheel opening moldings
Black body sill with bright molding
Roof drip moldings (Sport Coupe)
Bright taillight accents

The 1969 RS Convertible.

1969 Camaro Standard Equipment— Exterior

Front

Argent-colored plastic radiator grille

Bow tie radiator grille emblem

Valance-mounted parking lights (clear lens, amber light)

"Camaro by Chevrolet" header panel nameplate

Bright windshield reveal molding

Argent-colored headlamp bezels

Bright radiator grille outline molding

Side

Front and rear marker lamps (front amber, rear red)

White paint-filled front fender engine displacement numerals

"Camaro" front fender nameplate

Bright windshield pillar molding - convertible only

Hubcaps

Rocker molding

Left-hand outside rearview mirror

Rear

"Camaro by Chevrolet" deck lid nameplate

Rear bumper guards

Bright rear window reveal molding

Rear end panel mounted taillamps with bright bezels

Rear belt molding - convertible only

Back-up lamp mounted in taillamp unit

Bow tie rear end panel emblem

1969 Camaro Standard Equipment—Interior
Roof and Pillars

Prismatic ten-inch rearview mirror with padded edges
Satin-finished rearview mirror support
Trim-colored plastic rearview mirror support center
Padded sun visors
Padded, trim-colored windshield pillars
Plastic, trim-colored coat hooks (coupe only)
Bright bezeled center dome light (coupe only)
Bright front seat shoulder belt roof rail stowage clips (coupe only)
Plastic, trim-colored front seat shoulder belt anchor cover (coupe only)
Left and right door jamb switches

Seats and Floor Covering

All vinyl front bucket seats
All vinyl rear bench seat
Bright seat adjuster handle
Bright front seat back rear latches
Seat belts
Front seat shoulder belts (coupe only)
Luggage compartment spatter paint
Carpeted passenger compartment floor
All vinyl front seat head restraints

Door and Quarter Panel Trim

All vinyl door and quarter trim panel
Padded front door armrests
Silver-accented, clear plastic window regulator knobs
Bright door lock buttons
Rear quarter panel armrest with ashtray (convertible only)
"Camaro" door nameplate

Instrument Panel

Blended-air heater with lighted controls
"Camaro" nameplate (right side)
Bright cowl vent control knobs
Trim-colored instrument panel pad
Temperature, generator, oil pressure, and brake warning lights
Positive-type glove compartment door lock
High-beam and turn signal indicators
Two-speed windshield wiper with washer
Slide-type windshield wiper control
Ashtray mounted cigarette lighter
Astro-ventilation outlets (left and right side)
Bright, black accented light switch knob
Front passenger compartment courtesy lights
"Molded-in" clock cover

1969 Camaro Major Appearance and Performance Options
RPO Z87 Custom interior

Deluxe seat and sidewall trim
Additional body insulation
Molded trunk mat
Glove compartment lamp
Full molded hood insulation
Instrument panel wood grain
Bright pedal pad trim
Wood-grained steering wheel shroud
Right-hand instrument panel molding and assist handle

RPO Z23 Special Interior Group

Instrument panel wood grain
Bright pedal pad trim
Wood-grained steering wheel shroud
Right-hand instrument panel molding and assist handle

RPO Z22 Rally Sport

"RS" steering wheel emblem
Black steering wheel shroud (except when RPO Z87 or RPO Z23 is ordered)
Bright drip gutter molding (coupe only)
Black paint below rocker molding
Wheel opening moldings
Special black painted radiator grille (except on black exterior color cars)
Concealed headlights
Bright bezel around parking lights
"RS" grille and rear panel emblems
"Rally Sport" front fender nameplate
Wheel opening paint stripes (not on SS cars)
Bright rear quarter simulated louvers
Special taillights with bright horizontal bar on lens
Back-up lights in rear valance
Headlamp washer system

RPO Z21 Style Trim Group

Taillamp lens with bright vertical bars
Bright drip gutter molding (coupe only)
Black paint below rocker molding
Wheel opening moldings
Wheel opening paint stripes (except on SS cars)
Bright rear quarter simulated louvers
Bright headlamp bezel face moldings

RPO C06 Vinyl Roof

Vinyl top material
Roof, rear quarter, and tulip panel molding (coupe only)

Above, tail and backup light from 1969 RS.

Left, striping of the 1969 SS.

Below, standard interior from 1969 Camaro.

RPO Z27 Super Sport

Full molded hood insulation
"SS" steering wheel emblem
Black steering wheel shroud (except when combined with RPO Z87 or RPO Z23)
Taillamp lens with bright vertical bars
Black paint below rocker molding
Bright rear quarter simulated louvers
Front fender and door paint stripe
"SS" grille, front fender, and rear panel emblems
Black painted rear end panel (L34, L35, L78 only)
Special hood with simulated intakes
Front fender engine numerals
Bright engine chrome
F70-14-4 PR white lettered wide oval tires with 14"x7" wheels
Black painted radiator grille (except black exterior color cars)
Bright headlamp bezel face moldings

Super Sport and Rally Sport Options Combined

Full molded hood insulation
"SS" steering wheel emblem
Black steering wheel shroud (except RPO Z87 or RPO Z23)
Bright drip gutter molding (coupe only)
Black paint below rocker molding
Wheel opening moldings
Special black painted radiator grille (except black exterior color cars)
Concealed headlights
Bright bezel around parking lights
Bright rear quarter simulated louvers
Special taillights with bright horizontal bar on lens
Back-up lights in rear valance
Front fender and door paint stripe
"SS" grille, front fender, and rear panel emblems
Black painted rear end panel (L34, L35, L78 only)
Special hood with simulated intakes
Front fender engine numerals
Bright engine chrome
F70-14-4 PR white lettered wide oval tires with 14"x7" wheels
Headlamp washer system

1969 Camaro Factory and Dealer Options

RPO Z27
Camaro SS includes 300hp Turbo-Fire 350 V-8, special hood, sport striping, hood insulation, F70x14 wide-oval white lettered tires and 14"x7" wheels, special suspension, power disc brakes, special three-speed transmission, bright accents on simulated rear fender louvers, bright engine accents, and "SS" emblems................$281.00

RPO Z87
Custom interior includes molded vinyl door panels with built-in armrests, assist grip, carpeted lower panel, woodgrain accents on instrument panel and steering wheel, bright pedal trim, glove compartment light, special body insulation, and luggage compartment mat. $105.00

RPO Z23
Special Interior Group (included in Custom interior option) includes woodgrain accents on steering wheel and bright pedal trim. $17.00

RPO Z22
Rally Sport includes special grille with concealed headlights, headlight washers, fender striping, bright accents on simulated rear fender louvers, front and rear wheel opening moldings, black body sill, "RS" emblems on grille and rear panel, Rally Sport front fender nameplates, bright accented taillights and parking lights, back-up lights below rear bumper, "RS" emblem and black accents on steering wheel, and bright roof drip molding on Sport Coupe. $125.00

RPO Z21
Style Trim (included in Rally Sport option) includes fender striping, bright accents on simulated rear fender louvers, front and rear wheel opening moldings, black body sill, rear panel emblem, and bright taillight accents.
Convertible: $35.00

Sport Coupe (also includes bright roof drip molding): $45.00

RPO Z28
Special Performance Package (Z28) includes 302ci V-8 engine, dual exhaust with deep-tone mufflers, special front and rear suspension, rear bumper guards, heavy-duty radiator and temperature-controlled fan, quick-ratio steering, 15"x7" rally wheels, E70x15 special white-lettered tires, 3.73 ratio axle and special rally stripes on hood and

rear deck. Available only when four-speed transmission, power disc brakes are ordered. Available on Sport Coupe model only. Posi-traction rear axle recommended. $435.00

COPO 9561
Includes L72 427/425hp engine, ZL2 cowl induction hood system with L78 air cleaner, HD F62 front springs, and HD G32 five-leaf springs, 4.10 rear axle ratio with service package 12-bolt rear housing, and HD "curved-neck" radiator . .$489.75

COPO 9560
Includes ZL1 aluminum block 427/430hp engine, ZL2 special ducted hood, F41 heavy-duty springs, V01 heavy-duty radiator, G80 posi-traction rear axle with 4.10 gear ratio, and K66 transistorized ignition $4,160.15

COPO 9737
Sport Car Conversion includes 140 mph speedometer, 1" stabilizer shaft, and E70x15 Goodyear Wide Tread GT white letter tires $184.70
(Above COPO options did not appear on dealer information. These cars were extremely limited production factory race cars. Most dealers were not even aware of these option packages.)

Feature Groups
Appearance Guard Group
Includes:

A - Front bumper guards (RPO V31)	12.00
B - Rear bumper guards (RPO V32)	12.00
C - Door-edge guards (B93)	4.00
D - Color-keyed floor mats, two front and two rear (RPO B37)	11.00
E - Visor vanity mirror (RPO D34)	3.00
For all models without special rear springs - includes A, B, C, D, E (RPO ZP5)	42.00
For all models with special rear springs - includes A, C, D, E (RPO ZP5)	30.00

Operating Convenience Group
Includes:

A - Electric clock (included when special instrumentation is ordered; RPO U35)	15.00
B - left-hand outside remote-control rearview mirror (RPO D33)	10.00
C - Rear window defroster (RPO C50)	
Sport Coupe	21.00
Convertible	31.00
For Sport Coupe with special instrumentation - includes B, C (RPO ZQ2)	31.00

For Sport Coupe without special instrumentation -

includes A, B, C (RPO ZQ2)	46.00
For Convertible with special instrumentation - includes B, C (RPO ZQ2)	41.00
For Convertible without special instrumentation - includes A, B, C (RPO ZQ2)	56.00

** Any item contained in feature groups may be ordered separately.

Power Teams
Engines: See Power Teams section for model and transmission availability

155hp Turbo-Thrift 250 Six (RPO L22)	25.00
255hp Turbo-Fire 350 V-8 (RPO LM1)	50.00
325hp Turbo-Jet 396 V-8 (RPO L35 - available only with Camaro SS model option and ordering information)	60.00

Transmission: See Power Teams chart for availability

Torque-Drive (six-cylinder only - RPO MB1)	65.00
Powerglide (RPO M35)	
six-cylinder models	155.00
eight-cylinder models	165.00
Turbo Hydra-Matic (RPO M40)	180.00
Special three-speed (RPO MC1 - included with Camaro SS option)	75.00
Four-speed (wide-range - RPO M20)	185.00
Four-speed (close-ratio - RPO M21)	185.00
Four-speed (close-ratio - RPO M22)	322.10
Axle, Posi-traction Rear (RPO G80 - not available when Torque-Drive transmission is ordered)	40.00

Axle Ratios: See Power Teams chart for available combinations

Economy (RPO ZQ8)	2.00
Performance (RPO ZQ9)	2.00
Special Ratio (other than standard, economy, or performance)	2.00

Power Assists

Brakes, Power Drum (RPO J50)	40.00
Brakes, Power Disc Front (RPO J50/J52 - included with Camaro SS option)	61.00
Brakes, 4-wheel Power Disc (RPO JL8 - includes 15" wheels, available only for Camaro SS or Z28)	500.25
Steering, Power (RPO N40 - power brakes recommended)	90.00
Top, Power Convertible (RPO C06)	50.00
Windows, Power (RPO A31)	100.00

Other Options
Air Conditioning, Four Season (RPO C60 - not available when 302ci engine is ordered. Includes 61-amp Delcotron, heavy-duty radiator, and tem-

Wheel of 1969 SS.

perature-controlled fan. Power steering recommended) 357.00
Battery, Heavy-Duty (RPO T60) 8.00
Belts, Seat and Shoulder: In addition to or replacing seat belts
Standard Style Shoulder Belts
Convertible only
Two front (RPO AS1) 22.00
Two front, two rear (RPO AS1/AS5) 44.00
Sport Coupe
Two rear (RPO AS5) 22.00
Custom Deluxe Belts
Seat and Shoulder Belts
Sport Coupe with bucket seats - five seat and two shoulder (RPO ZK3) 11.50
Seat Belts Only
Convertible with bucket seats - five seat (RPO A39) 8.50
Shoulder Belts Only
Convertible (requires option A39)

Two front (RPO A85) 25.00
Two front, two rear (RPO A85/AS4) 50.00
Sport Coupe (requires option ZK3)
Two rear (RPO AS4) 25.00
Bumper, Special Front (RPO VE3 - not available with front bumper guards) 40.00
Clutch, Heavy-Duty: Dual Disc (RPO MA6 - Camaro SS only) N.C.
Console (RPO D55 - includes floor shifter, storage compartment, and ashtray) 51.00
Exhaust System, Dual (RPO N10 - available with 210hp or 255hp engine only) 29.00
Temperature-Controlled Fan (RPO K02 - V-8 models only, included with air conditioning or special performance package) 15.00
Generator:
42-amp Delcotron (RPO K79 - not available with air conditioning or special performance package) 10.00
63-amp Delcotron (RPO K85 - with air conditioning) 5.00

63-amp Delcotron (RPO K85 - without air conditioning) 25.00

Glass, Soft-Ray Tinted (RPO A01 - all windows) 31.00

Headlight Washer (RPO CE1 - included with Rally Sport equipment) 15.00

Heater, Engine Block (RPO K05) 10.00

Instrumentation, Special (RPO U17 - V-8 models with console only. Includes ammeter, temperature, oil pressure and fuel gauges mounted on console; electric clock and tachometer mounted in instrument cluster) 90.00

Light Monitoring System (RPO U46) 25.00

Lighting, Auxiliary
A - Ashtray Light
B - Courtesy Lights
C - Glove Compartment Light
D - Luggage Compartment Light
E - Under-hood Light

For Sport Coupe with Custom interior (RPO ZJ9 - includes A, B, D, E) 10.50

For Sport Coupe without Custom interior (RPO ZJ9 - includes A, B, C, D, E) 13.00

For Convertible with Custom interior (RPO ZJ9 - includes A, D, E) 6.50

For Convertible without Custom interior (RPO ZJ9 - includes A, C, D, E) 9.00

Radiator, Heavy-Duty (RPO V01 - included with conditioning; not available with 396ci engine or special performance package) 14.00

Radio Equipment
Radios, Pushbutton - with front antenna

AM Radio (RPO U63) 58.00

AM/FM Radio (RPO U69) 127.00

AM/FM Radio and Stereo (RPO U79) 227.00

Antenna, Manual Rear - not available with AM/FM or spoiler (RPO U73) 9.00

Speaker, Rear Seat - not available when stereo is ordered (RPO U80) 12.50

Roof Cover, Vinyl (RPO C08 - Sport Coupe models only)

Black (BB) 80.00

Dark Blue (CC) 80.00

Parchment (EE) 80.00

Midnight Green (SS) 80.00

Dark Brown (FF) 80.00

Seat, Fold Down Rear (RPO A67) 40.00

Shift Lever, Floor Mounted (RPO M11 - available with standard three-speed transmission and six-cylinder or standard V-8 engines; included with center console) 10.00

Speed Warning Indicator (RPO U55) 11.00

Springs, Heavy-Duty Rear (RPO G31 - includes rear bumper guards) 19.00

Spoiler, Air: Front and Rear (RPO D80) 31.00

Steering, Special (RPO N44 - includes quick-response steering; requires power steering when air conditioning or 396ci engine is ordered) 15.00

Steering Wheel, Comfortilt (RPO N33 - available only with automatic or floor-shift transmission) 43.00

Steering Wheel, Sport-Styled (RPO N34 - wood-grained plastic rim) 33.00

Stereo Tape System (RPO U57 - includes 4 speakers; not available with electric clock; console required when air conditioning is ordered) 127.00

Striping, Fender (RPO D96 - included with Rally Sport and Style Trim option) 15.00

Striping, Front Accent (RPO DX1 - not available with Sport Striping) 24.00

Striping, Sport (RPO D90 - included when Camaro SS is ordered; not available with Front Accent Striping) 24.00

Suspension, Special-Purpose Front and Rear (RPO F41 - V-8 models only; not available when Special Performance Package is ordered; includes special front and rear springs and shock absorbers) 10.00

Top, Convertible: Manual

White (AA) N.C.

Black (BB) N.C.

Two-Tone Finish: Sport Coupe only 30.00

Ventilation, HD Closed Positive Engine (RPO KD5) 6.00

Wheel Covers, Full (RPO P01 - not available when Special Performance Package is ordered) 20.00

Wheel Covers, Simulated Wire (RPO N95 - not available when Special Performance Package is ordered) 70.00

Wheel Covers, Mag-Style (RPO N96 - not available when Special Performance Package is ordered) 70.00

Wheel Covers, Mag-Spoke (RPO PA2 - not available when Special Performance Package is ordered) 70.00

Wheel Trim Rings: For use with standard hubcaps (RPO P06 - not available when Special Performance Package is ordered) N.A.

Wheels, Rally (RPO ZJ7 - includes special wheel, center cap, and trim ring. Not available when Special Performance Package is ordered) 34.00

Wheels, Sport (RPO N66 - available only with Camaro SS) 75.00

Factory Installed Regular Production Tubeless Tires

Replaces (five) E78x14 Original Equipment Blackwall

(five) E78x14 Original Equipment Whitewall (RPO PK8) 30.00

(five) F70x14 Special Red Stripe (RPO PW8) 60.00

Console for 1969.

Chambered exhaust on 1969 model.

Crossram-equipped 302 engine.

The 375hp 396ci engine option for 1969.

(five) F70x14 Special White Stripe (RPO PW7) 60.00
(five) F70x14 Special Belted Red Stripe (RPO PY5) 85.00
(five) F70x14 Special Belted White Stripe (RPO PY4)   85.00
(five) F70x14 Special Blackwall with White Lettering (RPO PL5)   60.00
Replaces (five) F70x14 Special Blackwall with White Lettering (Camaro SS)
(five) F70x14/2 ply (4-ply rating) Special Red Stripe (RPO PW8)   N.C.
(five) F70x14/2 ply (4-ply rating) Special White Stripe (RPO PW7)   N.C.
(five) F70x14/2 ply (4-ply rating) Special Belted Red Stripe (RPO PY5)   25.00
(five) F70x14/2 ply (4-ply rating) Special Belted White Stripe (RPO PY4)   25.00
Space Saver Spare Tire (RPO N65)   19.00

Canadian Options

Floor Mats (RPO B37)
Computer-Selected Front Springs (RPO F62)
Computer-Selected Rear Springs (RPO G32)

Canadian Specific/Only Options

Engine Coolant - Increased Protection, antifreeze (RPO V48)
Additional Fuel for Delivery (RPO W84)
Tire Pressure Sticker (RPO ZK8)
Canadian Warranty Booklet and miscellaneous literature (RPO ZQ7)

Mid-Year Options

Dual Chambered Exhaust System (RPO NC8)
Tachometer Gauge (RPO U16)
Liquid Tire Chain (RPO V75)
Cowl Induction Hood (RPO ZL2 - available only with SS or Z28)
Indy Sport Convertible Accents (RPO Z11)

Dealer-Installed Custom Features and Accessories

Description	Part No.
Air Conditioning	
GM Chevrolet - six-cylinder	987334
GM Chevrolet - eight-cylinder(except 396 and 427)	987335

GM Chevrolet - eight-cylinder(with 396 and 427)
987336

Air Conditioning Adapter
Must be ordered for any Camaro A/C installation
987322

Antennas
Right Front, AM/FM 31"   993632
Right Front, all except AM/FM   993631
Right Rear, except AM/FM   993683
Power Brakes
Except 396, J-50 option   993763
Locking Gasoline Tank Cap
All   987291
Electric Clocks
console mounted except RPO U17, U57, and A/C
993581
Polishing Cloth
12 cloths, 18"x32"   987570
100 cloths, Special Promotional Activities   987685
100 cloths, Special Christmas Activities   986035
Auto Compass, all models   987457
Litter Container, Saddle type, all except SS
Black   986607
Blue   986602
Fawn   986603
Red   986608
Wheel Covers, set of four, 14", option P01   987288
Wheel Covers, set of four, 14", Simulated Wire, option N95   987100
Cruise-Master
Eight-cylinder, auto transmission (307-327)993767
Defogger, Rear Window, except convertible, option C50   993514
Tissue Dispenser, Instrument Panel   987403
Fire Extinguisher, 2.75lb dry chemical type985592
Fire Extinguisher Recharge Kit   985593
Rear Bumper Guards, option V32   993510
Front Bumper Guards, option V31   993506

Door Edge Guards
2 door, option B93   993582
Fender Guard   993740
Trailer Wiring Harness   993589
Heater, Engine Block
Except 396 and 427 engines, option K05   993541
With 396 and 427 engines, option K05   993542
Highway Emergency Kit   986792

Lights
Ashtray, part of ZJ9 option   993580
Courtesy, part of ZJ9 option   993607
Glove compartment, part of ZJ9 option   987188
Luggage compartment, part of ZJ9 option   993551
Under-hood, part of ZJ9 option   993553
GM Vigilite, coupe, U46 option   993646
Spare Tire and Wheel Locks   987048
Contour Rubber Floor Mats, Front - Twins
Dark Blue, option ZP5 and B37   993611
Black, option ZP5 and B37   993610
Red, option ZP5 and B37   993614
Midnight Green, option ZP5 and B37   993667
Dark Green, option ZP5 and B37   993668
Outside Rearview Mirrors
Right Hand, Rectangular   993595
Vanity Visor Mirror
All, option D34   993723
Radio and Antenna
AM/FM with stainless front antenna, option U69
993637
Pushbutton with front antenna, option U63 993636
Seat Belt Retractor   986068
GM Child Safety Seat, Deluxe   987499
GM Child Safety Seat, Standard   993502
Speakers
Rear Seat, option U80   993538
Speaker Housing, rear   987280
Hand Portable Spotlamp
For use in any 12-volt cigarette lighter   987112
Stereo Multiplex
Basic Unit, option U79   993705
Stereo Multiplex (Installation Packages)
12000 series   993711
Tachometer
All eight-cylinder engines   993716
Tape Players
Basic Unit with D55 (includes installation package)   993702
Tape Player (Installation Package)
12000 series, except D55   993730
Tape Cartridge
Volume Two   993768
Volume One   987118
Covers (for tape player installation—two in carton)
993579

1969 Camaro Trim Plate

Early Type		
(Los Angeles and Norwood from N500001 to N544000)		
Body by Fisher		
ST 69 (A)		(B) BDY
TR (C)		(D) PNT
(E)		

NOR=Norwood, OH
LOS=Los Angeles, CA
3-5/16" X 1-3/4"

Late Type				
(Norwood from N544001 to end of production)				
Body by Fisher				
ST 69	(A)	NOR	(B) BDY	
TR	(C)		(D) PNT	
	(E)		(F)	

3-1/2" X 2-1/8"

Location A - Model Identification
12437 - V-8 coupe
12467 - V-8 convertible
12337 - six-cylinder coupe
12367 - six-cylinder convertible

Location B - Unit number and assembly plant code

Location C - Interior Trim Code
711 - Black standard
712 - Black custom
713 - Black Houndstooth
714 - Yellow Houndstooth
715 - Blue standard
716 - Blue custom
718 - Red standard
719 - Red custom
720 - Orange Houndstooth
721 - Medium Green standard
722 - Medium Green custom
723 - Midnight Green standard
725 - Midnight Green custom
727 - Ivory standard
729 - Ivory Houndstooth
A - White convertible top
B - Black convertible top

The Z28 striping pattern on this 1969 Z28 stopped just below the edge of the cowl vent panel.

A good view of the chambered exhaust option available on 1969 Camaros.

1969 Z28 front sway bar. Notice front spring tag (YF) on coil spring.

1969 307ci/200hp with smog equipment. The washer bottle location on this denotes it is a Rally Sport.

Location D - Body Color Code
10 - Tuxedo Black
50 - Dover White
51 - Dusk Blue
52 - Garnet Red
53 - Glacier Blue
55 - Azure Turquoise
57 - Fathom Green
59 - Frost Green
61 - Burnished Brown
65 - Olympic Gold
67 - Burgundy
69 - Cortez Silver
71 - LeMans Blue
72 - Hugger Orange
76 - Daytona Yellow
79 - Rallye Green
— - Special Paint
B - Black vinyl top
C - Blue vinyl top
E - Parchment vinyl top
F - Brown vinyl top
S - Green vinyl top

Location E - Time Built Code
01 - January
02 - February
03 - March
04 - April
05 - May
06 - June
07 - July
08 - August
09 - September
10 - October
11 - November
12 - December
A - 1st week of month
B - 2nd week of month
C - 3rd week of month
D - 4th week of month
E - 5th week of month

Location F - Exterior Trim Codes
X11 - Style Trim Group (includes SS350)
X22 - Style Trim Group with SS396 (black rear panel)

Hood pin and lanyard was used on crossram fiberglass
hooded cars in 1969.

X33 - Style Trim Group with Special Performance Equipment (Z28)

X44 - Base car

X55 - Base car with SS350 (rear fender louvers, black body sill*)

X66 - Base car with SS396 (rear fender louvers, black rear panel, black body sill*)

X77 - Base car with Special Performance Equipment (Z28)

Z11 - Indy Pace Car Accents

Z10 - Indy Pace Car Accents - Hardtop

D80 - Air Spoiler Equipment (when used - not all cars built with spoilers were coded)

Style Trim Group (included in Rally Sport option) consisted of fender striping (except when Sport Striping or Z28 is specified), and simulated rear fender louvers, front and rear wheel opening moldings, black body sill*, rear panel emblems, bright headlight and taillight accents. Sport coupe included bright roof drip moldings.

* Except colors 51, 57, 61, and 67.

Note: Camaro SS included rear fender louvers and black body sill*. Black rear panel was included with 396 engine. Z11 and Z10 included orange hood, deck, and fender striping and deleted the black body sill and rear panel with 396 engine.

1969 Camaro Protect-O-Plate

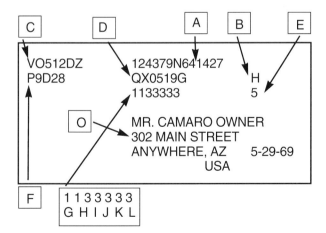

Location A - Model Identification

A five digit number will be used on all 1967-72 cars. The basic number group is 12000 series for Camaro. The first two digits denote the vehicle series. The third digit indicates base engine equipment, and the fourth and fifth digits identify the body style. When the third digit is an odd number, the base engine is an L-6. When the third digit is an even number, the base engine is a V-8. Therefore:

12347 - six-cylinder coupe

12367 - six-cylinder convertible

12437 - eight-cylinder coupe

12467 - eight-cylinder convertible

The complete serial number consists of the above model identification, year of manufacture, assembly plant designation, and sequence number. Example: 124379N647420

     12437 - V-8 Camaro Coupe

     9 - 1969

     N - Norwood

     647420 - Sequential Body Number

Camaro build sequence numbers begin at 500001 at the Norwood plant.

Assembly Plant Designations

N - Norwood

L - Los Angeles

Location B - Carburetor Source

Code-Plant

B - Bay City

C- Carter

H- Holley

R- Rochester

Location C - Engine Production Code Number Explanation

Example: VO512DZ

V - Plant

     V- Flint Motor

     F - Flint Motor

     T - Tonawanda Engine Plant

     K - McKinnon Industries

     V - Flint Engine

     S - Saginaw Service

05 - Month (May)

12 - Day (12th)

DZ - 302 Z/28

Engine plants will stamp a source, production date, and engine suffix on all engines.

Assembly plants will stamp assembly plant designation and continuous sequence number portion of the vehicle identification number on all 307, 327, 350, 396, and 427ci engines, except Corvette.

This big block is air-conditioned as evidenced by the rubber seal on top of the core support.

Engine Production Code Number Locations:
Passenger four or six-cylinder: stamped on pad right side of engine at rear of distributor.
Passenger V-8: tamped on pad immediately forward of right hand cylinder head.

1969 Engine Codes
AM - 230, Manual Transmission
AN - 230, Powerglide, torque-drive
AO - 230, three-speed, THM 350 Transmission
AP - 230, CAC
AQ - 230, Powerglide, torque-drive, CAC
AR - 230, three-speed THM 350 Transmission, CAC
BB - 250, Powerglide, torque-drive
BC - 250, Powerglide, torque-drive, CAC
BD - 250, three-speed THM 350
BE - 250, Manual Transmission
BF - 250, CAC
BH - 250, three-speed THM 350, CAC
DZ - 302, Z28
DA - 307, Manual Transmission
DC - 307, Powerglide

DD - 307, three-speed THM 350
DE - 307, four-speed Manual Transmission
FJ - 327, Manual Transmission
FK - 327, Powerglide
FL - 327, THM Transmission
HA - 350, Manual Transmission
HB - 350, three-speed THM
HC - 350, two-barrel
HD - 350, two-barrel, three-speed THM 350
HE - 350, Powerglide
HF - 350, two-barrel, Powerglide
HQ - 350, Manual Transmission
HR - 350, Powerglide
HS - 350, three-speed Auto Transmission
JB - 396, Powerglide
JF - 396 High Performance
JG - 396, three-speed THM 400
JH - 396 Special High Performance
JI - 396 High Performance, three-speed THM 400
JJ - 396, Aluminum Heads, Manual Transmission
JL - 396 Special High Performance, three-speed THM 400
JM - 396, Aluminum Heads, three-speed THM 400

A Yenko dealership-prepared 427 Camaro. This one is a
1969 beauty.

JU - 396, Manual Transmission

KA - 396 Special High Performance, Manual
Transmission

KC - 396 Special High Performance, Manual
Transmission

KE - 396, Aluminum Heads, Manual Transmission

MN - COPO 9561 427/425, four-speed Transmission

MO - COPO 9561 427/425, THM 400, Special
COPO/ZL1 conversion

ML - COPO 9560 427/430, four-speed Transmission

MM - COPO 9560 427/430, THM 400, Special
COPO/ZL1 conversion

MV - RPO ZL1 (added in April 1969) - prototype
for street detuned use (COPO 9567)

MX - RPO ZL1 (added in April 1969) - prototype
for street detuned use (COPO 9567)

Location D - Rear Axle Code

BA - 2.56
BB - 2.56 posi
BC - 3.36
BD - 3.36 posi
BE - COPO ZL1 HD 4.10
BI - 2.73
BL - 3.07
BM - 3.31
BN - 3.55
BO - 3.73
BP - 2.73
BQ - 2.73 posi
BR - 3.07 posi
BS - 3.31 posi
BT - 3.55 posi
BU - 3.73 posi
BV - 4.10 posi
BW - 4.56 posi
BX - 4.88 posi
DT - COPO 9560/9561 HD 4.56
PA - 3.08
PB - 2.56

1969 was the only year for cowl induction. The large rubber seal around the air cleaner fit the round opening in the hood. Hood insulation was cut around this hood opening.

PC - 2.56 posi
PE - 3.08 posi
PX - 2.73 posi
PZ - 2.56 posi
QN - 4.88 posi, 4-wheel
QS - 2.56 posi, 4-wheel discs
QT - 2.73 posi, 4-wheel
QV - 3.07 posi, 4-wheel
QW - 3.31 posi, 4-wheel discs
QX - 3.73 posi, 4-wheel
QY - 4.10 posi, 4-wheel
QZ - 4.56 posi, 4-wheel discs
01-12 Month
01-31 Day of Month
Plant Codes:
B - Buffalo
G - Chevrolet Gear and Axle
K - McKinnon Industries
W - Warren

Location E - Month of Vehicle Build
8 - August 1968
9 - September 1968
0 - October 1968
N - November 1968
D - December 1968
1 - January 1969
2 - February 1969
3 - March 1969
4 - April 1969
5 - May 1969
6 - June 1969
7 - July 1969

Nice view of the cowl induction hood and silver grill on this 1969 Z28.

Location F - Transmission Code

S - Saginaw three-speed
C - Cleveland Powerglide
M - Muncie three-speed
T - Toledo Powerglide
H - Muncie HD three-speed
E - McKinnon Industries Powerglide
K - McKinnon three-speed
A - Cleveland Torquedrive
R - Saginaw four-speed
B - Cleveland THM 350
P - Muncie four-speed
Y - Toledo THM 350
9 - Model Year (1969)

A-M: Month Produced
A - January
B - February
C - March
D - April
E - May
F - June
G - July
H - August
J - September
K - October
L - November
M - December
01-31 Day of Month

Turbo-Hydra-matic 400 - Production code number contains model year, model identification, and production date. Below the production date is the source serial number.
Example: 69C234

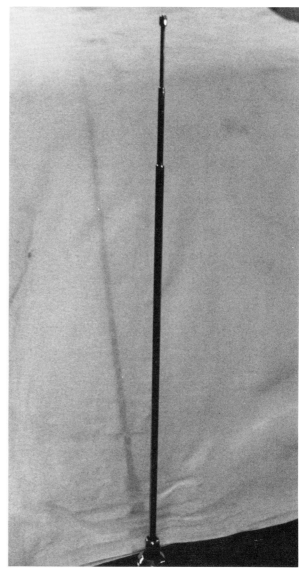

Original 1969 AM antenna. These were an oval, telescoping design.

69 - Model Year
C - Engine of Vehicle
234- Build Date Code
    C - 396/325hp
    E - 396/350
    X - 427/425 or 427/430
    Y - 396/375 with high shift point
The build date code for the 1969 model year starts with the first day of the calendar year 1968 and continues through the 1969 calendar year.
Example: Build date code 234 is for August 21, 1968 (the 234th day of that year). Build date code 367 is January 1, 1969 (there were 366 days in 1968 - leap year).

Location G - Power Steering Option
1 - N40 Power Steering

Location H - Power Brake Option
1 - J50 Power Brakes

Location I - Radio Code
3 - U63 Radio
3 - U69 AM/FM Radio
3 - U79 AM/FM Stereo Radio

Location J - Disc Brake Code
3 - J52 Disc Brakes

Location K - Air Conditioning Code
1 - C60 Air Conditioning
3 - C75 Comfortron

Location L - Power Window Code
3 - A31 Power Windows

Location M - Power Seat Option
Not available on Camaro

Location N - Chevrolet Bow tie Emblem

Location O - Dealer supplied owner information as shown in Dealer Policy and Procedure Manual.

If not for the license tag on this car, this 1969 COPO would look like any other plain-wrapper 1969 Camaro.

Twin 1969 Camaro Pace Cars on display. Both are 350-equipped.

1969 Camaro Pace Car. This car had no console. Note the shift boot and plate. Hurst shifter was a curved stick.

*1969 Camaro with big block powerplant. 1967-69 Camaros
with under-hood lamp had lamp mounted on passenger
side for big block and driver side for small block.*

Good view of pulley setup on this air conditioned, smog-equipped 1969 Camaro.

This photo of a 1969 Camaro shows spare tire placement.

Original 1969 Rally Sport headlight switch. These were different than standard cars because RS headlights were vacuum operated.

Door edge guards were available as a separate option in 1969, or as part of a package.

This switch sat on top of the vacuum tank on 1968 and 1969 Rally Sport Camaros.

Big block SS cars featured a black tail panel, on all but a few dark colored paint schemes.

Chapter 4

1970 Camaro

1970 Manufacturer's suggested retail price (MSRP) for base model Camaros

Model Number	Description	MSRP
12337	six-cylinder Sport Coupe	$2,479.00
12437	eight-cylinder Sport Coupe	2,839.00

Note: Manufacturer's suggested retail price **(MSRP)** includes the factory D&H charge (including federal excise tax) and recommended dealer delivery and handling charge. This price does not include transportation charges, state and local taxes, or any accessories or optional equipment that may be ordered.

Camaro Standard Equipment

Protective inner skirts at both front and rear wheel openings; flush-and-dry rocker panels; energy-absorbing steering column; seat belts with pushbutton buckles for all passenger positions; passenger-guard door locks with deflecting lock buttons on all doors; four-way hazard flasher; dual master cylinder brake system with warning light and corrosion-resistant brake lines; latches on folding seat backs; dual-speed windshield wipers and washers; outside rearview mirror; back-up lights; side marker lights and parking lights that illuminate with headlights; padded instrument panel, sun visors, windshield pillars; reduced-glare instrument panel top, inside windshield moldings, horn button, steering hub, and windshield wiper arms and blades; inside day-night mirror with deflecting base; lane change feature in direction signal control; safety armrests; thick-laminate windshield; soft, low-profile window control knobs and coat hooks; energy-absorbing seat backs; yielding door and window control handles; energy-absorbing instrument panel with smooth contoured knobs and levers; tire safety rim; safety door latches and hinges; uniform shift quadrant; energy-absorbing steering wheel; snag-resistant steering wheel hardware; fuel tank and filler pipe security; high-level ventilation system; built-in blended-air heater and defroster system; Magic-Mirror acrylic lacquer finish; curved solid tempered plate glass windows; two-key lock system; weather-shielded key locks; color-keyed interior trim; scuff-resistant plastic cowl side panels with molded-in ventilator grilles; quality interior features and appointments; full-view instrument panel with instruments and controls; and locking glove compartment.

Consult authorized Chevrolet Dealers or your Fleet Representative for information on accessories and extra cost of optional equipment not listed.

General Motors Corporation reserves the right to make changes at any time, without notice, in prices, colors, materials, equipment, accessories, specifications, and models, and to discontinue models.

Body Structure

All-welded, heavy-gauge steel body
Double-panel doors, hood, and deck lid
Counter-balanced hood and deck lid
Front and rear inner fenders for improved corrosion protection
Side-guard beam door structure
Cargo-guard all-steel luggage compartment bulkhead
Flush-and-dry rocker panels
Double panel roof

1970 SS Camaro.

Body Insulation

Double-cushioned rubber body mounts
Rubber-cushioned front sheet metal
Jute pad floor insulation
Roof rear quarter area mastic insulation
Fibrous blanket cowl kick panel insulation
Asphalt-impregnated board rear seat back insulation

Body Sealing

Windshield and rear window bonded to body for positive sealing
Formed rubber deck lid seal
Weather-tight solid rubber window sill seals

Body Features

Thick-laminate windshield
Dual-speed electric windshield wipers and windshield washers
High-level ventilation system
Built-in blended-air heater and defroster system
Magic-Mirror acrylic lacquer finish
Curved solid tempered plate glass side and rear windows
Two-key lock system with keyless locking of all doors
Weather-shielded key locks
Scuff-resistant plastic cowl side panels
Astro-Ventilation system and full door-glass styling

Serial Numbers and Identification
Vehicle Identification Number (VIN)
Six-cylinder example: 123870L500026
12387 - Model
0 - Model Year (1970)
L - Assembly Plant
      L - Van Nuys
      N - Norwood
500026 - Unit Number

Eight-cylinder example: 124870N500001
12487 - Model
0 - Model Year (1970)
N - Assembly Plant (Norwood)
500001 - Unit Number
Starting unit number is 500001 and up at each plant regardless of series.
Location: The Vehicle Identification Number (VIN) is stamped on the plate attached to the top left-hand of the instrument panel.

Transmission Identification
Example: QPS9E01D
QP - Type Designation
S - Source Designation
R3 - three-speed, L6 and V-8 engines
S - Muncie
WB - four-speed, V-8 engine
R - Muncie
UD - Powerglide, L6
UF - Powerglide, V-8
C - Cleveland
T - Toledo
GW - Turbo Hydra-matic, V-8
CK - Turbo Hydra-matic, V-8
B - Cleveland
Y - Toledo
— - Ypsilanti
0 - Model Year (1970)
E01D - Production Month and Date

Location
Three-speed: stamped on right-hand side of case in the upper forward corner.
Four-speed: stamped on top right side of case.
Powerglide, Torque Drive, Turbo Hydra-matic (Chevrolet): stamped on right-hand side of pan.
Turbo Hydra-matic: nameplate tag on right-hand side of case.
Month
A - January
B - February
C - March
D - April
E - May
H - June
K - July
M - August
P - September
R - October
S - November
T - December
The letter D or N following the date indicates day or night shift.
Engine Identification
Example: F1210CTB
F - Source Designation (Flint)
1210 - Production Month and Date
CTB - Type Designation
Types:
250ci six-cylinder
    CRF - Regular engine, three-speed
    CCM - Regular engine, Powerglide
    CCG - Regular engine, manual transmission
    CCK - Turbo 350, Taxi and Police
    CCZ - Regular engine, manual transmission
    CRG - Regular engine, manual transmission

307ci eight-cylinder
    CNC - Regular engine, three-speed
    CND - Regular engine, four-speed
    CNE - Regular engine, Powerglide
    CNF - Regular engine, Turbo Hydra-matic (Chev-rolet)

350ci eight-cylinder (RPO L65)
    CNI - Optional engine, four-speed, two-barrel carburetor
    CNN - Optional engine, Turbo Hydra-matic (Chevrolet)
350ci eight-cylinder (RPO L48)
    CNJ - Optional engine, four-speed, four-barrel carburetor
    CRE - Optional engine, Turbo Hydra-matic (Chevrolet)

350ci eight-cylinder (RPO Z28)
    CTB - Optional engine, four-speed, four-barrel carburetor
    CTC - Optional engine, Turbo Hydra-matic (Chevrolet)

402ci (SS 396ci eight-cylinder (RPO L34)
    CTX - Optional engine, four-speed, four-barrel carburetor
    CTW - Optional engine, Turbo Hydra-matic

Another 1970 Camaro SS.

Location
Six-cylinder engine is stamped on pad on right side of cylinder block to rear of distributor.
Eight-cylinder engine is stamped on pad at front right side of cylinder block.

Rear Axle Identification
Identification number is stamped on bottom left or right of axle tube adjacent to carrier housing.

1970 Camaro Standard Equipment—Exterior

Base Model
Header panel nameplate "C" and "Camaro"
Valance mounted parking lamp with clear lens and amber bulb
Single "Power Beam" headlamps
Bright headlamp bezel
Argent-colored one-piece radiator grille
Bright radiator grille outline molding
One-piece front bumper with dual bumper guards

License plate mounting provision in front center
Bright top and side windshield reveal molding
Two-speed windshield wipers and washers
Non-depressed park, argent-colored wiper arms and 16" blades
Front marker lamps with amber lens - no bezel
Rear marker lamps with red lens - no bezel
Engine displacement numerals on fender (only with 350 or 396 engines)
Front fender "Camaro" nameplate
Rectangular left-hand rearview mirror
Bright chrome flush door handles
Wide rocker panel molding - bright
Bright lower window sealing strip bead
Bright body lock pillar vertical seal retainer
Hubcaps
Deck lid "Camaro by Chevrolet" nameplate
Bright rear window reveal moldings
Dual rear end panel mounted taillamps and back-up lamps with bright outer bezel

Woodgrain shift plate on 1970 Camaro.

Style Trim (RPO Z21)
Header panel nameplate "C" and "Camaro"
Valance mounted parking lamp with bright bezel
Single "Power Beam" headlamps
Bright headlamp bezel
Argent-colored one-piece radiator grille
Bright radiator grille outline molding
One-piece front bumper with dual bumper guards
Front license plate mounting provision in center
Bright top and side windshield reveal molding
Two-speed windshield wipers and washers
Non-depressed park, argent-colored wiper arms and 16" blades
Bright hood and fender rear edge molding
Front marker lamps with amber lens - no bezel
Rear marker lamps with red lens - no bezel
Engine displacement numerals on fender (350 and 396 only)
Front fender "Camaro" nameplate
Rectangular left-hand rearview mirror
Body colored tape insert on flush door handles
Wide rocker panel molding - bright
Bright body lock pillar vertical molding
Bright roof moldings
Bright door belt reveal molding
Hubcaps
Deck lid "Camaro by Chevrolet" nameplate
Bright rear window reveal moldings
Taillamps and back-up lamps with dual concentric bright bezels

Rally Sport (RPO Z22)
Header panel nameplate "C" and "Camaro"
Special parking lamp adjacent to headlamp with bright bezel and ornament
Single "Power Beam" headlamps
Bright headlamp bezel
Special two-piece, black-painted radiator grille with argent-painted leading edges
Bright radiator grille outline molding
Individual right-hand and left-hand front bumpers; resilient grille frame with rubber-protected center section of bumper stock
License plate mounting provision at front right bumper
Bright top and side windshield reveal molding
Two-speed windshield wipers and washers
Concealed black chrome-finished wipers - articulated left blade and 18" wiper blades
Bright hood and fender rear edge molding
Front marker lamps with amber lens - no bezel
Rear marker lamps with red lens - no bezel
Engine displacement numerals on fender (350 and 396 only)

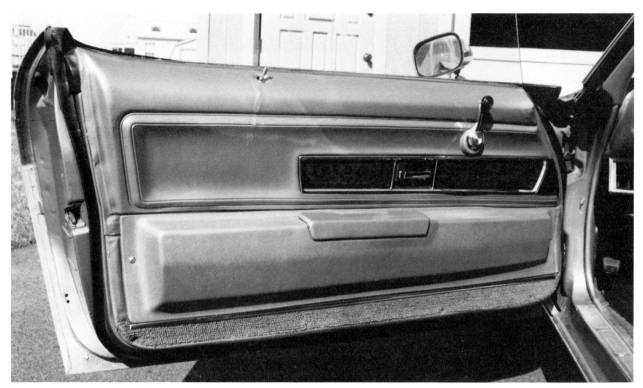

Deluxe door panel, circa 1970.

Deluxe interior, 1970.

Rally Sport fender nameplates
Rectangular left-hand rearview mirror
Body colored tape insert on flush door handles
Wide rocker panel molding - bright
Bright body lock pillar vertical molding
Hubcaps
Deck lid "Camaro by Chevrolet" nameplate
Bright rear window reveal moldings
Taillamps and back-up lamps with dual concentric bright bezels

Super Sport (RPO Z27)
Header panel nameplate "C" and "Camaro"
Valance mounted parking lamp with clear lens and amber bulb
Single "Power Beam" headlamps
Bright headlamp bezel
Black painted radiator grille
Bright radiator grille outline molding
Radiator grille "SS" emblem
One-piece front bumper with dual bumper guards
Front license plate mounting provision in center
Bright top and side windshield reveal molding
Two-speed windshield wipers and washers
Concealed black chrome-finished wipers - articulated left blade and 18" wiper blades
Front marker lamps with amber lens - no bezel
rear marker lamps with red lens - no bezel
Engine displacement numerals on fender (350 and 396 only)
"SS" front fender emblems
Rectangular left-hand rearview mirror
Bright chrome flush door handles
Wide rocker panel molding - bright
Bright lower window sealing strip bead
Bright body lock pillar vertical seal retainer
White lettered wide oval 14" tires on 14"x7" wheels
Hubcaps
Deck lid "Camaro by Chevrolet" nameplate
Bright rear window reveal moldings
Dual rear end panel mounted taillamps and back-up lamps with bright outer bezel
Black painted rear end panel (SS396 only)
Chrome-plated tailpipe ends - dual

Z28 (RPO Z28)
Header panel nameplate "C" and "Camaro"
Valance mounted parking lamp with clear lens and amber bulb
Single "Power Beam" headlamps
Bright headlamp bezel
Black painted radiator grille
Bright radiator grille outline molding
Radiator grille Z28 emblem

One-piece front bumper with dual bumper guards
Front license plate mounting provision in center
Wide hood paint stripes
Bright top and side windshield reveal molding
Two-speed windshield wipers and washers
Non-depressed park - argent-colored wiper arms and 16" blades
Front marker lamps with amber lens - no bezel
Rear marker lamps with red lens - no bezel
Z28 front fender nameplates
Rectangular left-hand rearview mirror
Bright chrome flush door handles
Wide rocker panel molding - bright
Bright lower window sealing strip bead
Bright body lock pillar vertical seal retainer
White lettered wide oval 15" tires on special 15"x7" wheels
Deck lid "Camaro by Chevrolet" nameplate
Bright rear window reveal moldings
Dual rear end panel mounted taillamps and back-up lamps with bright outer bezel
Z28 identification on spoiler
Deck lid spoiler
Wide paint stripes on deck lid and spoiler
Rear bumper guards
Chrome-plated tailpipe ends - dual

1970 Camaro Standard Equipment—Interior
Base Model
Trim color instrument panel pad
Bright accented black instrument cluster
Glove compartment door lock
"Camaro" glove compartment nameplate
Bright side kick-pad ventilation control knob
Bright Astro-ventilation control knob
T-handle parking brake release
Instrument panel Astro-ventilation outlets
Windshield wiper and washer switch (slide-type, depress to wash)
Bright lighting control knob with black accent
Speedometer, odometer, and fuel gauge
Temperature, generator, oil pressure, and brake warning telltale lights
Hi-beam and turn signal indicators
Automatic shift quadrant cover plate
Clock hole cover plate
Radio hole cover plate
Ashtray
Cigarette lighter
Blended-air heater with illuminated control plate
Black steering column
Black plastic oval two-spoke steering wheel
Black horn blowing shroud insert
Steering wheel shroud bow tie emblem

Steering column ignition switch with integral steering wheel and transmission lock
Black plastic hazard flasher knob
Black turn signal knob
Premier vinyl coated perforated headlining
Trim color windshield header, pillar, roof side rails, and rear window molding
Ten-inch prismatic rearview mirror with gray padded edges
Satin chrome finish mirror support, windshield mounted
Padded sunshades
Plastic coat hooks
Center dome lamp with bright bezel
Door jamb switches
Trim color front seat shoulder belt anchor covers
Front seat shoulder belt retainers, elastic and button
Bucket front seats - molded foam cushion and back
Rear seat - dual cushions with single, full-width backrest cotton padded
Bright front seat adjuster handle
Bright front bucket seat back latch
Passenger compartment floor carpet
Luggage compartment spatter paint
Front seat head restraints - trim color
Front and rear seat belts - four
Front shoulder belts - two
Front seat belt anchor covers
Door padded armrest
Built-in rear quarter panel armrest with ashtray
Clear blue tinted plastic window control handle knobs
Bright door lock buttons
Vinyl and plastic door and plastic quarter trim
Recessed door handle
Trim colored inside door handle cup and bezel
Black transmission shift lever knob
Floor-mounted transmission shift lever

Special Interior Group (RPO Z23)
Trim color instrument panel pad
Woodgrain appliqué on instrument cluster
Glove compartment door lock
"Camaro" glove compartment nameplate
Bright side kick-pad ventilation control knob
Bright Astro-ventilation control knob

1970 Camaro Standard Features
New vinyl roof and interior color choices
Sixteen Magic-Mirror acrylic colors (fourteen new)
New standard vinyl steering wheel
Hide-A-Way antenna built into windshield glass
Full foam seat construction replacing seat springs
New stronger front bumper

Occupant Protection Features
Seat belts with pushbutton buckles for all passenger positions
Single-buckle seat and shoulder belts for driver and right front passenger with reminder light and buzz-er
Two front seat head restraints
Energy-absorbing steering column
Passenger-guard door locks with forward mounted lock buttons
Safety door latches and hinges; folding seat back latches
Energy-absorbing padded instrument panel and front seat back tops
Thick-laminate windshield
Padded sun visors
Safety armrests
Safety steering wheel
Side-guard beams
Cargo-guard luggage compartment
Contoured full-roof inner panel
Full tank impact security
Glove compartment and console door latch impact security
Yielding windshield pillar moldings
Smooth-contoured door and window regulator handles
Soft, low profile window control knobs, coat hooks, and dome light
Stamped steel door hinges
High-strength front seat anchorages and construction
High-strength rear seat retention

Accident Prevention Features
Side marker lights and reflectors (front side marker lights flash with directional signal)
Parking lights that illuminate with headlights
Four-way hazard warning flasher
Back-up lights
Lane-change feature in direction signal control
Windshield defroster, washers, and dual-speed wipers
Wide-view inside day-night mirror (vinyl-edged, shatter-resistant glass) and deflecting support
Outside rearview mirror
Dual-action safety hood latches
Dual master cylinder brake system with warning light
Headlight aiming access provision
Low-glare instrument panel top, inside windshield moldings, wiper arms and blades, and steering wheel metallic surfaces
Safety wheel rims
Uniform shift quadrant

No winged wheel nuts, discs, and caps
Self-adjusting brakes
Starter safety switch
Improved bumper system
Illumination of windshield wiper and washer, heater and defroster controls

Anti-Theft Features
Anti-theft ignition key warning buzzer
Anti-theft steering column lock
Multiple key combinations
Visible vehicle identification
Tamper-resistant odometer with telltale feature

Traditional Quality Features
Astro-Ventilation system with large rectangular vent ports on instrument panel
Side marker lights front and rear
Long hood styling
Slender full-width front bumper, silver-finish grille in large grid pattern, license plate mounting centered between front bumper guards, and wide parking lights below bumper
Single-unit "Power Beam" headlights recessed in bright frames on front fenders
Wide body sill moldings
Flush mounted door handles
Recessed door handles
Swept-back roof and rear deck styling
Strato-bucket seats standard equipment
Wide (ten-inch) inside day-night rearview mirror
Outer front seat belt retractors
Acoustically engineered double-panel roof structure
Forward-mounted door lock buttons
Magic-Mirror acrylic lacquer finish
Flush-and-dry rocker panels
Curved side windows
Flush-mounted windshield and rear window bonded to body
Dual-speed electric windshield wipers
Built-in blended-air heater and defroster system
Inner fenders front and rear
108" wheelbase
Foot-operated parking brake
Deep-twist carpet floor covering
Suspended accelerator pedal
Efficient valve-in-head design
Positive-shift starter
Quiet hydraulic valve lifters
Sealed side-terminal Energizer battery
Automatic choke on all engines
Advanced accessory drive system on all V-8 engines

Trim plate for 1970 Camaro.

Delcotron generator
Seven main bearing six-cylinder engine with fully counterweighted crankshaft
Transmission-controlled spark advance
Separate front frame unit
Advanced design front suspension with forward-mounted steering linkage
Wide front and rear tread
Bias belted ply tires
Bias-mounted rear shock absorbers (curb side unit mounted ahead of axle, other mounted behind) for excellent suspension control
Computer-selected front and rear springs
Independent coil front suspension
Multi-leaf rear springs
Disc brakes standard on front wheels (power operation optional)
Finned rear brake drums; Self-adjusting brakes
Precise Ball-Race steering

1970 Camaro Specifications
Interior Roominess

Head room - front	37.4
Head room - rear	36.1
Leg room - front	43.8
Leg room - rear	29.6
Hip room - front	56.7
Hip room - rear	47.3
Shoulder room - front	56.7
Shoulder room - rear	54.4
Front entrance height	29.6

Glass Area

Windshield glass area, sq. in.	1137.6
Rear window glass area, sq. in.	1099.2
Total glass area, sq. in.	3326.2

Protect-O-Plate for 1970 Camaro.

Tire Size and Steering Specifications

Standard tire size	E78x14
Turning circle - curb to curb, ft.	38.86
Turning circle - wall to wall, ft.	41.06
Steering ratio - power, overall	15:1

Fuel Capacity and Weight

Rated fuel tank capacity (gallons	19
Curb weight - L6, lbs.	3165
Curb weight - V-8, lbs.	3279
Shipping weight - L6, lbs.	3058
Shipping weight - V-8, lbs.	3172

1970 Camaro Options and Accessories
When Factory Installed

V-8 Models (200hp Turbo-Fire 307 V-8)

12487 Sport Coupe	$2,839.00

Six-cylinder Models (155hp Turbo-Thrift 250 Six)

12387 Sport Coupe	2,749.00

Camaro SS
Includes 300hp Turbo-Fire 350ci engine and bright accents; power brakes, special ornamentation; special hood insulation; F70-14 bias belted ply white lettered tires, 14"x7" wheels; black-painted grille; Hide-A-Way windshield wipers with black-chrome finished arms and articulated left-hand blade; "SS" emblems on steering wheel, fenders, grille and rear deck (V-8 model with four-speed manual or Turbo Hydra-matic transmissions only) . .$289.65

L34 350hp Turbo-Jet 396ci V-8 . . . .$152.75

L78 375hp Turbo-Jet 396ci V-838 . . . .$5.50

Z87
Custom interior: includes deluxe seat and sidewall trim; glove compartment light and additional in-strument cluster lighting; wood-grained accents on instrument cluster, steering wheel and door trim panels; luggage compartment mat plus special engine compartment, hood and interior insulation (with cloth or vinyl seats) $115.90

Z23
Accent Group Interior: includes additional instrument cluster lighting, wood-grained accents on instrument cluster and steering wheel (included in Custom interior option) $21.10

Z22
Rally Sport: includes special black painted grille with special rubber tipped vertical center bar and resilient body color grille frame; independent left-hand and right-hand front bumpers replacing full-width bumper; license plate bracket mounted below right-hand bumper; parking lights with bright accents mounted on grille panel; Hide-A-Way windshield wipers with black-chrome finished arms and articulated left-hand blade; bright window, hood panel and body sill moldings; body colored insert on door handles; "RS" emblem on steering wheel, grille, and rear deck lid; Rally Sport front fender nameplates; bright accented taillights and back-up lights (Rally Sport emblems deleted with Camaro SS or Z28 Special Performance Package; available only with F78-14 or F70-14 tires) $168.55

Z21
Style Trim: includes body colored insert on door handles, bright window, body sill, and hood panel moldings plus bright accented parking lights, taillights, and back-up lights (included with Rally Sport option) $52.70

Z28
Special Performance Package: includes special 360hp 350ci engine with bright accents; heavy-duty radiator; dual exhausts; black painted grille; Z28 emblems on grille, front fenders, and rear deck lid; rear bumper guards; special performance suspension; heavy-duty front and rear springs; 15"x7" wheels with bright lug nuts, special center caps, and trim rings; special hood insulation; F60-15B bias-belted ply white lettered tires, rear deck spoiler, and special paint stripes on hood and rear deck (V-8 model only; available only with special instrumentation, four-speed manual or Turbo Hydra-Matic transmission, power brakes, and Positraction rear axle) $572.95

Feature Groups

ZP5   Appearance Guard Group includes:
B93   Door Edge Guards   5.30
B37   Trim Color Twin Front and Rear Floor Mats   11.60
D34   Vanity Visor Mirror   3.20
ZJ9   Auxiliary Lighting Group includes:
   Courtesy Lights
   Glove Compartment Light
   Luggage Compartment Light
   Under-hood Light
   Ashtray Light   13.70
   with Custom Interior Group   11.10
ZQ2   Operating Convenience Group includes:
U35   Electric Clock   15.80
D35   Exterior Sport Mirrors   26.35
C50   Forced-air Rear Window Defroster   26.35

Power Teams

Engines: See Power Team chart for complete engine specifications, model, and transmission availability
L65   250hp Turbo-Fire 350ci V-8 (with F78-14 or F70-14 tires only)   31.60
Transmissions: See Power Team chart for availability
M35   Powerglide automatic (standard engines only)   174.25
M40   Turbo Hydra-matic automatic (V-8 models only; $221.80 with 350hp Camaro SS engine; $290.40 with Z28 Special Performance Package)   200.65
M20   Four-speed wide-range Transmission (250, 300, 350, 360, 375hp engines only)   205.95
G80   Posi-traction Rear Axle   44.25

Axle Ratios

YD1   Special axle ratio for trailering   12.65
ZQ9   Performance axle ratio (available only with 375hp engine or Z28 Special Performance Package and posi-traction rear axle)   12.65

Power Assists

J50   Power Brakes, for use with standard manual disc type front brakes (included with Camaro SS)   47.40
N40   Power Steering, variable ratio (power brakes recommended)   105.35

Other Options

C50   Rear Window Defroster, forced air   26.35
C60   Air Conditioning, Four Season: includes heavy-duty radiator (V-8 models only; power steering recommended; not available with 375hp Ca-

1970 AM/FM front and rear speaker radio.

maro SS engine or Z28 Special Performance Package)   380.25
D80   Spoiler, Rear Deck (included with Z28 Special Performance Package; a different spoiler was also available with the Z28 Special Performance Package as COPO 9796 at $36.90)   32.65
T60   Battery, Heavy-Duty; 15-plate, 80 amp-hr   15.80

Belts

AK1   Belts, Custom Deluxe, five seat and two front shoulder (replaces standard belts)   12.15
AS4   Belts, Rear Shoulder, for use with Custom Deluxe belts   26.35
D55   Console: includes floor-mounted shift lever (when automatic transmission is ordered), compartment and ashtray   59.00
A01   Glass, Soft Ray tinted, all windows   37.95
U14   Special Instrumentation; includes tachometer, ammeter, and temperature gauges plus electric clock mounted in instrument panel cluster (V-8 models only)   84.30
Radio Equipment
U63   AM Radio, pushbutton   61.10
U69   AM/FM Radio, pushbutton   133.80
U80   Rear Seat Speaker   14.75
C08   Vinyl Roof Cover, includes bright metal roof outline moldings (BB - black, GG - green, AA - white)   89.55
N33   Comfortilt Steering Wheel   45.30
F41   Special Suspension, special performance front and rear, includes special front stabilizer and special shock absorbers (V-8 models only; included with 350hp or 375hp Camaro SS engine or Z28 Special Performance Package)   30.55
NA9   Emission Control, evaporative (released to conform with California registration requirements)   36.90
C24   Windshield Wipers; Hide-A-Way, includes articulated left-hand blade (included with Rally Sport or Camaro SS)   19.00

D34   Vanity Visor Mirror   3.20

D35   Exterior Sport Mirrors, includes right-hand mirror and remote-controlled left-hand mirror   26.35

U35   Electric Clock, included with special instrumentation   15.80

VF3   Bumpers; deluxe front and rear, includes slender black resilient front and rear bumper cushions and rear bumper guards ($24.25 with Z28 Special Performance Package)   36.90

V01   Heavy-Duty Radiator (included with air conditioning or Z28 Special Performance Package)   14.75

PL3   Tires, E78-14/B bias belted ply white stripe   26.05

PL4   Tires, F70-14/B bias belted ply white letter, includes 14"x7" wheels (included with Camaro SS)   65.35

PX6   Tires, F78-14/B bias belted ply white stripe   43.30

PY4   Tires, F70-14B bias belted ply white stripe (includes 14"x7" wheels)   65.70

P01   Wheel Covers, bright metal (not available with Special Performance Package)   26.35

P02   Wheel Covers, special (not available with Special Performance Package)   79.00

ZJ7   Wheels, Rally; includes special 14"x7" wheels, hubcaps, and trim rings (available only with F70-14 tires)   42.15

Dealer-Installed Custom Features and Accessories

Description	Part No.
Air Conditioning	
six-cylinder Camaro	987334
eight-cylinder Camaro, except 396	987335
eight-cylinder Camaro with 396	987336
Air Conditioning Installation and	
Adapter Package, Camaro	987322
Antenna	
AM/FM Front	993632
Right Front AM	993631
Right Rear AM	993683
Power Brakes, Nova and Camaro	993763
Child Safety Seat, Deluxe	987499
Child Safety Seat, Standard	993502
Electric Clock, floor mounted	993581
Locking Gas Cap	987291
Compass	993915
Forced Air Rear Window Defogger	993514
Fire Extinguisher	985592
Fire Extinguisher Recharge Kit	985593
Door Edge Guards	993582
Highway Emergency Kit	993537
Infant Safety Seat	993970
Lights	
Courtesy	993607
Glove Compartment	987188
Luggage Compartment	993551
Under-hood	993553
Liquid Tire Chain	993814
Deck Lid Luggage Carrier	993645
Luggage Carrier Cover	987053
Floor Mats, trim color twin	
Front - Black	993610
Rear - Black	993615
Front - Blue	993836
Rear - Blue	993844
Floor Mats, color keyed twin front and rear	
Front - Green	993839
Rear - Green	993847
Front - Gold	993838
Rear - Gold	993846
Front - Red	993841
Rear - Red	993849
Front - Saddle	993837
Rear - Saddle	993845
Front - Sandalwood	993843
Rear - Sandalwood	993851
Vanity Visor Mirror	993723
AM Radio with antenna	993636
AM/FM Radio with antenna	993637
Front Speakers, pair	993565
Rear Speaker, left-hand location only	993538
Hand Portable Spotlight	987112
Tissue Dispenser and Litter Container	
Black	986607
Blue	986602
Fawn	986603
Red	986608
Wheel Covers, 14" Camaro	987288
Wheel Covers, Mag-Style Wheel Covers, 14" Camaro	993986
Wheel Covers, Simulated Wire Wheel Covers, 14" Camaro	987067
Front Bumper Guards	993506
Rear Bumper Guards	993510
Fender guards, pair	993740
Deluxe Tissue Dispenser and Litter Container	993920
Engine Block Heater, except 396 and 427	993541
Engine Block Heater, with 396 and 427	993542
Spare Tire and Wheel Locks	987048
Outside Rearview Mirror, right-hand	993595
Demountable Ski Rack, rain-gutter type	993782
Windshield Washer Fluid Monitor	993921
Stereo Tape Player	993654

| Stereo Tape Player with console | 993702 |
| Tape Cartridge Holder | 993579 |

1970 Camaro Trim Plate

```
ST 70(A) -12487(B)    NOR(C)    182953(D) BODY
TR 713(E)             43(F) 43(G)  PNT
05D (H)                          Z28 (I)
```

Location A - Model Year
70 - 1970

Location B - Body Style
12387 - six-cylinder Coupe
12487 - eight-cylinder Coupe

Location C - Assembly Plant
NOR - Norwood, Ohio
LOS - Van Nuys, California

Location D - Sequential Body Number
The number assigned to that particular body at the assembly plant

Location E - Interior Trim Code
710 - Sandalwood standard vinyl
711 - Black standard vinyl
712 - Black custom vinyl
713 - Black/White pattern custom cloth
714 - Black/Blue pattern custom cloth
715 - Blue standard vinyl
716 - Blue custom vinyl
720 - Black/Green pattern custom cloth
723 - Green standard vinyl
724 - Green custom vinyl
725 - Black custom cloth
726 - Saddle standard vinyl
727 - Saddle custom vinyl

Location F - Lower Body Paint Code
10 - Classic White
14 - Cortez Silver
17 - Shadow Gray
25 - Astro Blue
26 - Mulsanne Blue
43 - Citrus Green
45 - Green Mist
48 - Forest Green
51 - Daytona Yellow
53 - Camaro Gold
58 - Autumn Gold
63 - Desert Sand
65 - Hugger Orange
67 - Classic Copper
75 - Cranberry Red

Location G - Upper Body Paint Code
A number here would designate no vinyl top. The number should match the lower body color.
BB - Black
AA - White
GG - Dark Green

Location H - Build Date Code
01 - January
02 - February
03 - March
04 - April
05 - May
06 - June
07 - July
08 - August
09 - September
10 - October
11 - November
12 - December
A - 1st week of month
B - 2nd week of month
C - 3rd week of month
D - 4th week of month
E - 5th week of month

Location I - Option Code
(Norwood cars only) - No designation here would tell you only that the car is not a Norwood Z28.
Z28 - RPO Z28

1970 Camaro Protect-O-Plate

```
                    123870N123456(A)       H(B)
F1210CTB(C)         COZ0227G(D)            W(E)
P7B26(F)            1(G)1(H)4(I)3(J)4(K)5(L)1(M)
                                           (N)

                    Chevrolet Owner
                    123 Main St.
                    Anywhere, AB      3-15-70
                              USA
```

A Protect-O-Plate was furnished with all 1970-72 Camaros. This was a metal plate imprinted at the assembly plant and contained information on various standard or optional equipment. You may determine from the imprinted information on the plate the type of engine, transmission, rear axle, exterior color, the month the vehicle was produced, and other basic vehicle information.

There was no Protect-O-Plate furnished with 1973 and up Camaros.

Location A - Vehicle Identification Number
12487 - Sport Coupe, V-8 engine
12387 - Sport Coupe, six-cylinder
N - Plant (Norwood)
L - Plant (Los Angeles)
123456 - Sequential Body Number

Location B - Carburetor Source
B - Bay City
C - Carter
H - Holley
R - Rochester

Location C - Engine Production Code
F - Flint
K - McKinnon Industries
S - Saginaw
T - Tonawanda
V - Flint Engine Plant
1-12 Month Production Code:
1 - January
2 - February
3 - March
4 - April
5 - May
6 - June
7 - July
8 - August
9 - September
10 - October
11 - November
12 - December
01-31 Day of Month

1970 Engine Codes:
250/155hp
CCM - Powerglide, Police and Taxi
CCG - Manual Transmission
CCK - Turbo Hydra-matic 350, Police and Taxi
CCZ - Manual Transmission
CCL - Manual Transmission, Police and Taxi
CRF - Manual Transmission
CRG - Manual Transmission

307/200hp
CNC - Manual Transmission
CND - four-speed Manual Transmission
CNE - Powerglide
CNF - Turbo Hydra-matic 350

350
CNI - 350/250 Manual Transmission
CNJ - 350/300 Manual Transmission
CNK - 350/300 Powerglide
CRE - 350/300 Turbo Hydra-matic 350
CNM - 350/250 Powerglide
CNN - 350/250 Turbo Hydra-matic 350
CTB - 350/360 Manual Transmission
CTC - 350/360 Turbo Hydra-matic 400

396
CJL - 396/375 Turbo Hydra-matic 400
CJF - 396/350 Manual Transmission
CJH - 396/375 Manual Transmission
CJI - 396/350 Turbo Hydra-matic 400
CTX - 396/350 (L34) four-speed, four-barrel carburetor
CTW - 396/350 (L34) Turbo Hydra-matic

Location D - Rear Axle Code
COC - 2.73
COD - 2.73 posi
COE - 3.08
COF - 3.08 posi
COO - 4.10
COS - 3.07
COT - 3.07 posi
COU - 3.31
COV - 3.31 posi
COX - 3.55 posi
COZ - 3.73 posi
CRI - 3.08 posi
CRX - 2.73
CRY - 2.73 posi
01-12 Month
01 - January
02 - February
03 - March
04 - April
05 - May
06 - June
07 - July
08 - August
09 - September
10 - October
11 - November
12 - December
01-31 Day of Month

1970 RS Z/28 featured low rear spoiler.

Plant Codes:
B - Buffalo
G - Chevrolet Gear and Axle
K - McKinnon
W - Warren

Location E - Month of Vehicle Build
D - December 1969
1 - January 1970
2 - February 1970
3 - March 1970
4 - April 1970
5 - May 1970
6 - June 1970
7 - July 1970
8 - August 1970
9 - September 1970

Location F - Transmission Number
D - Saginaw three-speed OD
K - McKinnon Industries four-speed
C - Cleveland Powerglide

The 1970 interior was unique to that one particular year. Low-backed buckets with separate headrests were replaced in 1971 by high-backed buckets with separate headrests were replaced in 1971 by high-backed buckets with integral headrests.

M - Muncie three-speed
R - Saginaw four-speed
T - Toledo Powerglide
K - McKinnon Industries three-speed
P - Muncie four-speed
E - McKinnon Industries Powerglide
H - Muncie Heavy-Duty
A - Cleveland Torque Drive
X - Cleveland THM 350
B - Cleveland THM 350
Y - Toledo THM 350
0 - Model Year (1970)
A-T Calendar Month:
A - January
B - February
C - March
D - April
E - May
H - June
K - July
M - August
P - September
R - October
S - November
T - December
01-31 Day of Month
Turbo Hydra-matic Code: Contains model year, model identification, and production date
70 - Year 1970

Engine Identification:
E - 396/350hp
C - 396/325hp (Chevelle/Camaro)
Y - 396/375hp
Build Date: Code of 1970 model year begins with first day of the calendar year 1969 and continues through the 1970 calendar year.

Location G - Power Steering
1 - N40 Power Steering only

Location H - Power Brakes
1 - J50 Power Brakes

Location I - Radio Option
3 - U63 AM Radio

This 1970 Camaro still has the smog equipment. Notice the canister in front next to upper radiator hose. What a nightmare of hoses!

3 - U69 AM/FM

Location J - Disc Brake Option
3 - J52 Disc Brakes

Location K - Air Conditioning Option
1 - C60 Air Conditioning

Location L - Power Window Equipment Option
Power windows were not available on 1970 Camaros

Location M - Power Seat Option
Power seats were not available on 1970 Camaro

Location N - Chevrolet Bow tie Emblem

Chapter 5

1971 Camaro

Front end of the 1970-71 Z28.

1971 Manufacturer's suggested retail price (MSRP) for base model Camaros

Model Number	Description	MSRP
12387	six-cylinder Sport Coupe	$2,758.00
12487	eight-cylinder Sport Coupe	2,848.00

Note: Manufacturer's suggested retail price **(MSRP)** includes the factory D&H charge (including federal excise tax) and recommended dealer delivery and handling charge. This price does not include transportation charges, state and local taxes, or any accessories or optional equipment that may be ordered.

Camaro Standard Equipment

Protective inner skirts at both front and rear wheel openings; flush-and-dry rocker panels; energy-absorbing steering column; seat belts with pushbutton buckles for all passenger positions; passenger-guard door locks with deflecting lock buttons on all doors; four-way hazard warning flasher; dual master cylinder brake system with warning light and corrosion-resistant brake lines; latches on folding seat backs; dual-speed windshield wipers and washers; outside rearview mirror; back-up lights; side marker lights and parking lights that illuminate with headlights; padded instrument panel, sun visors, and windshield pillars; reduced-glare instrument panel top, inside windshield moldings, horn button, steering hub, and windshield wiper arms and blades; inside day-night mirror with deflecting base; lane change feature in direction signal control; safety armrests; thick-laminate windshield; soft, low-profile window control knobs and coat hooks; energy-absorbing seat backs; yielding door and window control handles; energy-absorbing instrument panel with smooth contoured knobs and levers; tire safety rim; safety door latches and hinges; uniform shift quadrant; energy-absorbing steering wheel; snag-resistant steering wheel hardware; fuel tank and filler pipe security; high-level ventilation system; built-in blended-air heater and defroster system; Magic-Mirror acrylic lacquer finish; curved solid tempered plate glass windows; two-key lock system; weather-shielded key locks; color-keyed interior trim; scuff-resistant plastic cowl side panels with molded-in ventilator grilles; quality interior features and appointments; full-view instrument panel with instruments and controls; and locking glove compartment.

General Motors Corporation reserves the right to make changes at any time, without notice, in prices, colors, materials, equipment, accessories, specifications, and models, and to discontinue models.

Body Structure

All-welded, heavy-gauge steel body
Double-panel doors, hood and deck lid
Counter-balanced hood and deck lid
Front and rear inner fenders for improved corrosion protection
Side-guard beam door structure
Cargo-guard all-steel luggage compartment bulkhead
Flush-and-dry rocker panels
Double panel roof

Body Insulation

Double-cushioned rubber body mounts
Rubber-cushioned front sheet metal
Jute pad floor insulation
Roof rear quarter area mastic insulation
Fibrous blanket cowl kick panel insulation
Asphalt-impregnated board rear seat back insulation

Body Sealing

Windshield and rear window bonded to body for positive sealing
Formed rubber deck lid seal
Weather-tight solid rubber window sill seals

Body Features

Thick-laminate windshield
Dual-speed electric windshield wipers and windshield washers
High-level ventilation system
Built-in blended-air heater and defroster system
Magic-Mirror acrylic lacquer finish
Curved solid tempered plate glass side and rear windows
Two-key lock system with keyless locking of all doors
Weather-shielded key locks
Scuff-resistant plastic cowl side panels
Astro-Ventilation system and full door-glass styling

Serial Numbers and Identification
Vehicle Identification Number (VIN)
six-cylinder example: 123871L500001
12387 - Model
1 - Model Year (1971)
L - Assembly Plant (Van Nuys)
500001 - Unit Number
Therefore: The 25th model built at Van Nuys would be serial number 123871L500026

Eight-cylinder example: 124871N500001
12487 - Model
1 - Model Year (1971)
N - Assembly Plant (Norwood)
500001 - Unit Number
Therefore: The 1st model built at the Norwood plant would be serial number 124871N500001.

Assembly Plants
L - Van Nuys
N - Norwood
Starting unit number is 500001 and up at each plant regardless of series.
Location: The vehicle identification number (VIN) is stamped on the plate attached to the top left-hand of the instrument panel.

Transmission Identification
Example: S1E01
S - Source Designation
1 - Model Year 1971
E - Month of Production
01 - Day of Month

Source Designation
S - Muncie
R3 - three-speed, L6 engine
R4 - three-speed, V-8 engine
R - Muncie
WN - four-speed, V-8 engine
TH - Powerglide, L6 engine
TJ - Powerglide, V-8 engine
C - Cleveland
E - McKinnon Industries
HW - Turbo Hydra-matic, V-8 engine
CY - Turbo Hydra-matic, V-8 engine
B - Cleveland
Y - Toledo
— - Ypsilanti

Month
A - January
B - February
C - March
D - April
E - May
H - June
K - July
M - August
P - September
R - October
S - November
T - December
The letter D or N following the date indicates the day or night shift (on automatic only).

Location:
Three-speed: stamped on left-hand side just below cover.
Four-speed: stamped on top right side of case at adapter.
Powerglide, Torque Drive, Turbo Hydra-matic (Chevrolet): stamped on right-hand side of pan.
Turbo Hydra-matic: nameplate tag on right-hand side of case.

Engine Identification
Example: F1210CGP
F - Source Designation
12 - Production Month
10 - Production Day
CGP - Type Designation
Types:
250ci six-cylinder
    CAA - Regular engine, three-speed
    CAB - Regular engine, Powerglide

307ci eight-cylinder
    CCA - Regular engine, three-speed
    CCC - Regular engine, Powerglide
    CCC - Regular engine, Turbo Hydra-matic (Chevrolet)

350ci eight-cylinder (RPO L65)
    CGA - Optional engine, four-speed, two-barrel carburetor
    CGC - Optional engine, Turbo Hydra-matic (Chevrolet)

350ci eight-cylinder (RPO L48)
    CGP - Optional engine, four-speed, four-barrel carburetor
    CGR - Optional engine, Turbo Hydra-matic (Chevrolet)

350ci eight-cylinder (RPO Z28)
    CGP - Optional engine, four-speed, four-barrel carburetor

Standard door panel for the 1970-71 Camaro.

CGR - Optional engine, Turbo Hydra-matic (Chevrolet)

402ci (SS 396), eight-cylinder (RPO LS3)
 CLA - Optional engine, four-speed, four-barrel carburetor
 CLB - Optional engine, Turbo Hydra-matic

Location:
Six-cylinder engine is stamped on pad on right side of cylinder block to rear of distributor.
Eight-cylinder engine is stamped on pad at front right side of cylinder block.

Rear Axle Identification
Identification number is stamped on bottom left or right of axle tube adjacent to carrier housing.

1971 Camaro Standard Equipment— Exterior
Base Model
Header panel nameplate "C" and "Camaro"
Valance mounted parking lamp with clear lens and amber bulb
Single "Power Beam" headlamps
Bright headlamp bezel
Argent-colored one-piece radiator grille
Bright radiator grille outline molding
One-piece front bumper with dual bumper guards
License plate mounting provision in front center
Bright top and side windshield reveal molding
Two-speed windshield wipers and washers
Non-depressed park, dull-chrome wiper arms and 16" blades
Front marker lamps with amber lens - no bezel

Remote mirror option for the 1970-71 Camaro.

Rear marker lamps with red lens - no bezel
Engine displacement numerals on fender (only with 350 or 396 engines)
Front fender "Camaro" nameplate
Rectangular left-hand rearview mirror
Bright chrome flush door handles
Bright wide rocker panel molding
Bright lower window sealing strip bead
Bright body lock pillar vertical seal retainer
Hubcaps
Deck lid "Camaro by Chevrolet" nameplate
Bright rear window reveal moldings
Dual rear end panel mounted taillamps and back-up lamps with bright outer bezel

Style Trim (RPO Z21)
Header panel nameplate "C" and "Camaro"
Valance mounted parking lamp with clear lens and amber bulb
Single "Power Beam" headlamps
Bright headlamp bezel
Argent-colored one-piece radiator grille
Bright radiator grille outline molding
One-piece front bumper with dual bumper guards
License plate mounting provision in front center
Bright top and side windshield reveal molding
Two-speed windshield wipers and washers
Non-depressed park, dull-chrome wiper arms and 16" blades
Bright hood and fender rear edge molding
Front marker lamps with amber lens - no bezel
Rear marker lamps with red lens - no bezel

Engine displacement numerals on fender (only with 350 or 396 engines)
Front fender "Camaro" nameplate
Rectangular left-hand rearview mirror
Body colored tape insert on flush door handles
Bright wide rocker panel molding
Bright body lock pillar vertical molding
Bright roof moldings
Bright door belt reveal molding
Hubcaps
Deck lid "Camaro by Chevrolet" nameplate
Bright rear window reveal moldings
Taillamps and back-up lamps with dual concentric bright bezels

Rally Sport (RPO Z22)
Header panel nameplate "C" and "Camaro"
Special parking lamp adjacent to headlamp with bright bezel and ornament
Single "Power Beam" headlamps
Bright headlamp bezel
Special two-piece, black-painted radiator grille with argent-painted leading edges
Bright radiator grille outline molding
Individual right-hand and left-hand front bumpers; resilient grille frame with rubber-protected center section of bumper stock
License plate mounting provision at front right bumper
Bright windshield and rear window reveal molding
Two-speed windshield wipers and washers
Concealed black chrome-finished wipers - articulated left blade and 18" wiper blades
Bright hood and fender rear edge molding
Front marker lamps with amber lens - no bezels
Rear marker lamps with red lens - no bezels
Engine displacement numerals on fender (350 and 396 only)
Rally Sport fender nameplates
Rectangular left-hand rearview mirror
Body colored tape insert on flush door handles
Wide rocker panel molding - bright
Bright body lock pillar vertical molding
Bright roof moldings
Bright door belt reveal molding
Hubcaps
Deck lid "Camaro by Chevrolet" nameplate
Taillamps and back-up lamps with dual concentric - bright bezels

Super Sport (RPO Z27)
Header panel nameplate "C" and "Camaro"
Valance mounted parking lamp with clear lens and amber bulb

Single "Power Beam" headlamps
Bright headlamp bezel
Black painted radiator grille
Bright radiator grille outline molding
Radiator grille "SS" emblem
One-piece front bumper with dual bumper guards
Front license plate mounting provision in center
Bright windshield and rear window reveal molding
Two-speed windshield wipers and washers
Concealed black chrome-finished wipers - articulated left blade and 18" wiper blades
Front marker lamps with amber lens - no bezel
Rear marker lamps with red lens - no bezel
Engine displacement numerals on fender (350 and 396 only)
"SS" front fender emblems
Rectangular left-hand rearview mirror
Bright chrome flush door handles
Wide rocker panel molding - bright
Bright lower window sealing strip bead
Bright body lock pillar vertical seal retainer
White lettered wide oval 14" tires on 14"x7" wheels
Hubcaps
Deck lid "Camaro by Chevrolet" nameplate
Dual rear end panel mounted taillamps and back-up lamps with bright outer bezel
Black painted rear end panel (SS396 only)
Chrome-plated tailpipe ends - dual

Z28 (RPO Z28)
Header panel nameplate "C" and "Camaro"
Valance mounted parking lamp with clear lens and amber bulb
Single "Power Beam" headlamps
Bright headlamp bezel
Black painted radiator grille
Bright radiator grille outline molding
Radiator grille Z28 emblem
One-piece front bumper with dual bumper guards
Front license plate mounting provision in center
Wide hood paint stripes
Bright top and side windshield reveal molding
Two-speed windshield wipers and washers
Non-depressed park - dull chrome wiper arms and 16" blades
Front marker lamps with amber lens - no bezel
Rear marker lamps with red lens - no bezel
Z28 front fender nameplates
Rectangular left-hand rearview mirror
Bright chrome flush door handles
Wide rocker panel molding - bright
Bright lower window sealing strip bead
Bright body lock pillar vertical seal retainer

White lettered wide oval 15" tires on special 15"x7" wheels
Deck lid "Camaro by Chevrolet" nameplate
Bright rear window reveal moldings
Dual rear end panel mounted taillamps and back-up lamps with bright outer bezel
Z28 identification on spoiler
Deck lid spoiler
Wide paint stripes on deck lid and spoiler
Rear bumper guards
Chrome-plated tailpipe ends - dual

1971 Camaro Standard Equipment—Interior

Base Model

Trim color instrument panel pad
Bright accented black instrument cluster
Glove compartment door lock
"Camaro" glove compartment nameplate
Bright side kick-pad ventilation control knob
Bright Astro-ventilation control knob
T-handle parking brake release
Instrument panel Astro-ventilation outlets
Windshield wiper and washer switch (slide-type, depress to wash)
Lighting control knob - black with symbol
Speedometer, odometer, and fuel gauge
Temperature, generator, oil pressure, and brake warning telltale lights
Hi-beam and turn signal indicators
Automatic shift quadrant cover plate
Clock hole cover
Radio hole cover
Ashtray
Cigarette lighter knob - black with symbol
Blended-air heater with illuminated control plate
Black steering column
Black plastic oval two-spoke steering wheel with soft black shroud and decorative insert (entire top surface horn blowing pad).
Steering wheel shroud Chevrolet emblem
Steering column ignition switch with integral steering wheel and transmission lock
Black plastic hazard flasher knob
Soft black turn signal knob
One low-note horn
Premier vinyl coated perforated headlining
Trim color windshield header, pillar, roof side rails, and rear window moldings
Ten-inch prismatic rearview mirror with gray padded edges
Argent-painted rearview mirror support, windshield mounted

Padded sunshades
Plastic coat hooks
Center dome lamp with bright bezel
Door jamb switches
Black front seat shoulder belt anchor covers
Front seat shoulder belt retention - bright clip and clear plastic hanger
Bucket front seats with integral head restraints
Rear seat - dual cushions with single, full-width backrest cotton padded
Black front seat adjuster handle
Bright front bucket seat back latch
Passenger compartment floor carpet
Luggage compartment spatter paint
Front and rear seat belts - four
Front shoulder belts - two
Door padded armrests
Built-in rear quarter panel armrests
Clear plastic window control handle knobs
Bright door lock buttons
Vinyl and plastic door and plastic quarter trim
Recessed door handles
Trim colored inside door handle cup and bezel
Soft black transmission shift lever knob with white shift pattern
Floor-mounted transmission shift lever

Special Interior Group (RPO Z23)

Trim color instrument panel pad
Woodgrain appliqué on instrument cluster
Glove compartment door lock
"Camaro" glove compartment nameplate
Bright side kick-pad ventilation control knob
Bright Astro-ventilation control knob
T-handle parking brake release
Instrument panel Astro-ventilation outlets
Windshield wiper and washer switch (slide-type, depress to wash)
Lighting control knob - black with symbol
Speedometer, odometer, and fuel gauge
Temperature, generator, oil pressure, and brake warning telltale lights
Hi-beam and turn signal indicators
Glove compartment lamp
Automatic shift quadrant cover plate
Clock hole cover
Radio hole cover
Ashtray
Cigarette lighter knob - black with symbol
Blended-air heater with illuminated control plate
Black steering column
Black plastic oval two-spoke steering wheel with soft black shroud and decorative insert. Entire top surface horn blowing pad.

1970-71 4-speed console shift plate.

Woodgrain horn blowing shroud insert (insert is black if RS).

Steering wheel shroud Chevrolet emblem (emblem is replaced by RS if RS of RS/Z28 option is ordered)

Steering column ignition switch with integral steering wheel and transmission lock

Black plastic hazard flasher knob

Soft black turn signal knob

Argent-finish accent beads on lower instrument panel

One low-note horn

Premier vinyl coated perforated headlining

Trim color windshield header, pillar, roof side rails, and rear window moldings

Ten-inch prismatic rearview mirror with gray padded edges

Argent-painted rearview mirror support, windshield mounted

Padded sunshades

Plastic coat hooks

Center dome lamp with bright bezel

Door jamb switches

Black front seat shoulder belt anchor covers

Front seat shoulder belt retention - bright clip and clear plastic hanger

Bucket front seats with integral head restraints

Rear seat - dual cushions with single, full-width backrest cotton padded

Black front seat adjuster handle

Bright front bucket seat back latch

Passenger compartment floor carpet

Luggage compartment spatter paint

Front and rear seat belts - four

Front shoulder belts - two

Door padded armrests

Built-in rear quarter panel armrests

Clear plastic window control handle knobs

Bright door lock buttons

Vinyl and plastic door and plastic quarter trim

Recessed door handles

Trim colored inside door handle cup and bezel

Soft black transmission shift lever knob with white shift pattern

Floor-mounted transmission shift lever

Custom interior (RPO Z87)

Trim color instrument panel pad

Woodgrain appliqué on instrument cluster

Glove compartment door lock

"Camaro" glove compartment nameplate

Bright side kick-pad ventilation control knob

Bright Astro-ventilation control knob

T-handle parking brake release

Instrument panel Astro-ventilation outlets

Windshield wiper and washer switch (slide-type, depress to wash)

Lighting control knob - black with symbol

Speedometer, odometer, and fuel gauge

Temperature, generator, oil pressure, and brake warning telltale lights

Hi-beam and turn signal indicators

Glove compartment lamp

Automatic shift quadrant cover plate

Clock hole cover

Radio hole cover

Ashtray

Cigarette lighter knob - black with symbol

Blended-air heater with illuminated control plate

Black steering column

Black plastic oval two-spoke steering wheel with soft black shroud and decorative insert. Entire top surface horn blowing pad.

Woodgrain horn blowing shroud insert

Steering wheel shroud Chevrolet emblem (replaced by RS if RS or RS/Z28 option is ordered)

Steering column ignition switch with integral steering wheel and transmission lock

Black plastic hazard flasher knob

Soft black turn signal knob

Argent-finish accent beads on lower instrument panel
One low-note horn
Premier vinyl coated perforated headlining
Trim color windshield header, pillar, roof side rails, and rear window moldings
Ten-inch prismatic rearview mirror with gray padded edges
Argent-painted rearview mirror support, windshield mounted
Padded sunshades
Plastic coat hooks
Center dome lamp with bright bezel
Door jamb switches
Black front seat shoulder belt anchor covers
Front seat shoulder belt retention - bright clip and clear plastic hanger
Bucket front seats with integral head restraints
Deluxe seat trim
Rear seat - dual cushions with single, full-width backrest cotton padded
Black front seat adjuster handle
Bright front bucket seat back latch
Passenger compartment floor carpet
Luggage compartment rubber floor mat
Front and rear seat belts - four
Front shoulder belts - two
Door padded armrests
Built-in rear quarter panel armrests
Clear plastic window control handle knobs
Bright door lock buttons
Vinyl and plastic door and plastic quarter trim
Woodgrain insert on door trim panel with bright die-cast perimeter moldings
Recessed door handles
Trim colored inside door handle cup and bezel
Additional body insulation
Full molded hood insulation
Cowl-to-fender seal
Soft black transmission shift lever knob with white shift pattern
Floor-mounted transmission shift lever

New Features for 1971

New vinyl roof color choices
New softer instrument panel knobs
New interior color choices
Fifteen Magic-Mirror acrylic colors (eleven new) includes four exclusively for Camaro
New, high back bucket seats with built-in head restraints
New standard steering wheel with cushioned center. Optional steering wheels include the luxurious Custom or Sport with 4-spoke styling.

Slim-line spark plugs
New engine mounts now included with six as well as all V-8 power teams
Evaporation control system now standard equipment

Occupant Protection Features

Seat belts with pushbutton buckles for all passenger positions
Shoulder belts with pushbutton buckles driver and right front passenger
Two front seat head restraints
Energy-absorbing steering column
Passenger-guard door locks with forward mounted lock buttons
Safety door latches and hinges
Folding seat back latches
Energy-absorbing instrument panel and front seat back tops
Contoured roof rails
Thick-laminate windshield
Padded sun visors
Safety armrests
Safety steering wheel
Side-guard beams
Cargo-guard luggage compartment

Accident Prevention Features

Side marker lights and reflectors (front side marker lights flash with directional signal)
Parking lights that illuminate with headlights
Four-way hazard warning flasher
Back-up lights
Lane-change feature in direction signal control
Windshield defroster, washers, and dual-speed wipers
Wide-view inside day-night mirror (vinyl-edged, shatter-resistant glass)
Outside rearview mirror
Dual-action safety hood latches
Dual master cylinder brake system with warning light
Starter safety switch

Anti-Theft Features

Anti-theft ignition key warning buzzer
Anti-theft steering column lock

Traditional Quality Features

Astro-Ventilation system with large rectangular vent ports on instrument panel
Side marker lights front and rear
Long hood styling
Slender full-width front bumper, silver-finish grille

Several original documents available are shown with this 1971 Camaro.

in large grid pattern, license plate mounting centered between front bumper guards, wide parking lights below bumper

Single-unit "Power Beam" headlights recessed in bright frames on front fenders

Wide body sill moldings

Flush mounted door handles

Recessed door handles

Swept-back roof and rear deck styling

Strato-bucket seats standard equipment

Wide (ten-inch) inside day-night rearview mirror bonded to windshield glass

Outer front seat belt retractors

Acoustically engineered double-panel roof structure

Forward-mounted door lock buttons

Magic-Mirror acrylic lacquer finish

Flush-and-dry rocker panels

Curved side windows

Flush-mounted windshield and rear window bonded to body

Dual-speed electric windshield wipers
Built-in blended-air heater and defroster system
Inner fenders front and rear
108" wheelbase
Foot-operated parking brake
Deep-twist carpet floor covering
Suspended accelerator pedal
Efficient valve-in-head design
Positive-shift starter
Quiet hydraulic valve lifters
Sealed side-terminal Energizer battery
Automatic choke on all engines
Advanced accessory drive system on all V-8 engines
Delcotron generator
Seven main bearing, six-cylinder engine with fully counter-balanced crankshaft
Transmission-controlled spark advance
Separate front frame unit
Advanced design front suspension with forward-mounted steering linkage
Wide front and rear tread
Bias belted ply tires
Bias-mounted rear shock absorbers (curb side unit mounted ahead of axle, other mounted behind) for excellent suspension control
Computer-selected front and rear springs
Independent coil front suspension
Multi-leaf rear springs
Disc brakes standard on front wheels (power operation optional)
Finned rear brake drums
Precise Ball-Race steering
Self-adjusting brakes

1971 Camaro Options and Accessories
When Factory Installed
V-8 Models (200hp Turbo-Fire 307 V-8)
12487 Sport Coupe $2,848.00
Six-cylinder Models (145hp Turbo-Thrift 250 Six)
12387 Sport Coupe   2,758.00

Camaro SS
Includes 270hp Turbo-Fire 350ci engine with bright accents; dual exhausts; power brakes; left-hand remote control sport mirror; special ornamentation; special hood insulation; F70-14 bias belted ply white lettered tires; 14"x7" wheels; black finished grille; Hide-A-Way windshield wipers; and "SS" emblems on steering wheel and fender (V-8 model with four-speed and Turbo Hydra-Matic transmission only) $313.90

LS3 245hp Engine Turbo-Jet 396ci V-8 .... $99.05

Z87
Custom interior: includes deluxe seat and side-wall trim; cloth seats; glove compartment light and additional instrument cluster lighting; wood-grained accents on instrument cluster, steering wheel and door trim panels; luggage compartment mat plus special engine compartment, hood, and interior insulation $115.90

Z23
Accent Group Interior: includes additional instrument cluster lighting, wood-grained accents on instrument cluster and steering wheel (included in Custom interior option) $21.10

Z22
Rally Sport: includes special black finished grille with special rubber tipped vertical center bar and resilient body color grille frame; independent left-hand and right-hand front bumpers replacing full-width bumper; parking lamps with bright accents mounted on grille panel; Hide-A-Way windshield wipers, bright roof drip, window, hood panel; "RS" emblem on steering wheel; Rally Sport front fender nameplates; bright accented taillights and back-up lights (Rally Sport emblems deleted with Camaro SS or Z28 Special Performance Package) $179.05

Z21
Style Trim: includes bright roof drip, window and hood panel moldings, plus bright accented parking lights, taillights, and back-up lights (included with Rally Sport option) $57.95

Z28
Special Performance Package: includes special 330hp Turbo-Fire 350ci engine with bright accents; left-hand remote control sport mirror; special instrumentation; power brakes; 3.73 ratio Posi-traction rear axle; heavy-duty radiator; dual exhausts; black finished grille; Z28 emblems on front fenders; rear bumper guards; sport suspension; heavy-duty front and rear springs; 15"x7" wheels with bright lug nuts, special center caps, and trim rings; F60-15/B bias belted ply white lettered tires; rear deck spoiler with Z28 decal; and special paint stripes on hood and rear deck $786.75

Feature Groups

ZP5 Appearance Guard Group includes
B93   (A) Door Edge Guards   6.35
B37   (B) Color-keyed Front and Rear Floor Mats
                  12.65
D34   (C) Vanity Visor Mirror   3.20
ZJ9   Auxiliary Lighting: includes ashtray, courtesy, luggage compartment, under-hood, and glove compartment lights   1.45
      with Custom interior Group   15.80
ZQ2 Operating Convenience Group includes
      (A) Electric clock   16.90
      (B) Rear Window Defroster   31.60

Power Teams

Engines: See Power Team chart for complete engine specifications, model, and transmission availability
L65   245hp Turbo-Fire 350ci V   826.35
Transmissions: See Power Team chart for availability
M35   Powerglide automatic (standard engines only)   179.55
M40   Turbo Hydra-matic automatic (V-8 models only) with standard, 245hp or 270hp Camaro SS engine   216.50
      with 300hp Camaro SS engine   237.60
      with Z28   306.25
M20   Four-speed wide-range Transmission (available only when optional engine is ordered)   205.95
M21   Four-speed close-ratio Transmission (available only when 300hp Camaro SS engine or Z28 is ordered)   205.95
M22   Special four-speed close-ratio Transmission (available only with Z28)   237.60
G80   Posi-traction Rear Axle (included with Z28)   44.25
Note: This price increased to 46.35 during the year
Axle Ratios:
ZQ9   Performance Axle Ratio (available only when Z28 is ordered)   12.65
YD1   Trailering Axle Ratio (available only when 200hp or 240hp engine and Turbo Hydra-matic are ordered)   12.65

Power Assists

J50   Power Brakes (for use with standard manual disc/drum brakes. Included when Camaro SS or Z28 is ordered)   47.30
N40   Power Steering; variable-ratio (power brakes recommended)   110.60
Note: This price increased to 115.90 during the year

Other Options

C50   Rear Window Defroster   31.60
C60   Air Conditioning, Four-Season: includes heavy-duty radiator and 61-amp generator (V-8 models only; not available with Z28 Special Performance Package; price increased to $407.60 during the year)   402.35
D80   Spoiler, Front and Rear: includes front valance spoiler, rear deck, and rear side panel spoiler; front spoiler shipped loose for dealer installation   79.00
      with Z28 Special Performance Package, replaces rear deck spoiler only   46.35
T60   Heavy-Duty Battery, 80 amp-hr   15.80
AK1   Custom Deluxe Seat and Shoulder Belts: five seat and two front shoulder, includes brushed metal buckles and color keyed belts (replaced standard belts which were black)   15.30
AS4   Rear Shoulder Belts, for use with Custom Deluxe Belts   26.35
AN6   Adjustable Seat Back, two positions (driver's side only)   19.00
VF3   Deluxe Front and Rear Bumpers: includes slender black resilient front and rear bumper cushions and rear bumper guards   36.90
      with Z28 Special Performance Package 24.25
D55   Console: includes floor-mounted shift lever when automatic transmission is ordered, compartment and ashtray; also includes simulated wood-grained accents when Custom interior or Interior Accent Group is ordered   59.00
A01   Soft-Ray Tinted Glass, all windows 40.05
A02   Tinted Windshield   19.00
U14   Special Instrumentation: V-8 model only. Includes tachometer, ammeter, and temperature gauges plus electric clock mounted in instrument panel cluster, and additional instrument cluster lighting (included with Z28 Special Performance Package)   84.30
D35   Sport Mirror: left-hand remote control (included with Camaro SS or Z28 Special Performance Package)   15.80
V01   Heavy-Duty Radiator: V-8 models only, included with air conditioning or Z28 Special Performance Package   14.75
U63   AM Radio   66.40
U69   AM/FM Radio   139.05
U80   Rear Seat Speaker   15.80
C08   Vinyl Roof Cover, includes bright metal roof outline moldings AA - White, BB - Black, CC - Dark Blue, FF - Dark Brown, GG - Dark Green 89.55
N33   Comfortilt Steering Wheel   45.30
NK2   Custom Steering Wheel   15.80
NK4   Sport Steering Wheel (4-spoke)   15.80

F41   Sport Suspension (V-8 models with F70x14 tires only): included when 300hp Camaro SS engine or Z28 is ordered. Includes special front and rear stabilizer, special rear shock absorbers   30.55

P01   Wheel Covers, bright metal (not available with Z28 Special Performance Package)   26.35

P02   Special Wheel Covers (not available with Z28 Special Performance Package)   84.30

ZJ7   Rally Wheels, includes special 14"x7" wheels, hub- caps, and trim rings (not available with E78-14 tires)   45.30

C24   Hide-A-Way Windshield Wipers, includes articulated left-hand blade (included with Rally Sport or Camaro SS   21.10

Factory Installed Regular Production Tubeless Tires

Replaces (five) E78x14 bias belted ply blackwall (all models without Z28)

PL3   (five) E78-14B bias belted ply white stripe (not available when Camaro SS is ordered) Note: price increased to $28.15 during the year   26.05

PL4   (five) F70-14 bias belted ply white lettered. V-8 model only. Included when Camaro SS is ordered, includes 14"x7" wheels   81.50
Note: price increased to $83.60 during the year

PY4   (five) F70-14B bias belted ply white stripe, includes 14"x7" wheels (V-8 models only; no charge with Camaro SS) Note: price increased to $70.15 during the year   68.05

Dealer-Installed Custom Features and Accessories

Description	Part No.
Front Radio Antenna, AM and AM/FM	994128
Power Brakes	993989
Locking Gas Cap	994171
GM Child Safety Seat, Standard	993502
GM Child Safety Seat, Deluxe	987499
GM Infant Safety Carrier	993970
Rear Deck Lid Luggage Carrier	993862
Luggage Carrier Cover	987053
Electric Clock, floor mounted	993963
Compass	993915
Litter Container, Saddle-type	
Black	986607
Blue	986602
Fawn	986603
Red	986608
Wheel Covers, 14"	994138
Wheel Covers, 14" Coolie-Hat	993815
Wire Wheel Covers, 14"	987100
Simulated Magnesium Wheel Covers, 14"	993722
Rear Window Defogger	994182

Description	Part No.
Deluxe Tissue Dispenser and Litter Container	993920
Fire Extinguisher	994177
Fire Extinguisher Recharge Kit	985593
Rear Bumper Guards	993972
Door Edge Guards	993964
Fender Guards, front or rear, pair	993985
Trailer Wiring Harness	994131
Engine Block Heater, except 396 and 454	994161
Engine Block Heater, with 396 and 454	994162
Frame Mounted Trailer Hitch	994170
Highway Emergency Kit	993537
Lights	
Ashtray	994008
Glove Compartment	993982
Luggage Compartment	993997
Under-hood	993553
Hood Pin Locks with key	NPN
Contour Floor Mats	
Black, front	994033
Black, rear	994034
Dark Blue, front	994046
Dark Blue, rear	994050
Medium Beige, front	994047
Medium Beige, rear	994051
Dark Jade, front	994076
Dark Jade, rear	994077
Dark Saddle, front	994080
Dark Saddle, rear	994081
Right-hand Rearview Mirror	994039
Vanity Visor Mirror	993723
Demountable Ski Racks	994069
AM/FM Stereo Radio/Tape Player Combination	994113
AM Radio/Tape Player Combination	994112
AM/FM Pushbutton Radio	993931
AM Pushbutton Radio	993930
AM Radio/Tape Combination Replacement	994096
AM/FM Stereo Radio/Tape Combination Replacement	994097
CB Radio	2234214
CB Power Supply for Base Station	2234218
CB Antenna Body - Roof or Cowl Mount	2234327
CB Antenna Gutter Clamp Mount	2234217
CB Antenna Base Station	2234221
Seat Belt Buckle Retainers	994000
Rear Speakers	994121
Hand-Portable Spotlight	987112
8-track Tape Cartridge Holder	993579

1971 Camaro Trim Plate

```
┌─────────────────────────────────────────────┐
│              Body by Fisher                   │
│  ST 71 (A) 12487 (B)    NOR (C)   171489 BDY (D) │
│  TR 775 (E)         53 (F) -53(G)        PNT     │
│  04E (H)            Z27 (I)                      │
│              GENERAL MOTORS                     │
└─────────────────────────────────────────────┘
```

Location A - Model Year
71 - 1971

Location B - Body Style
12487 - Sport Coupe

Location C - Assembly Plant
NOR - Norwood, Ohio
BL - Van Nuys, California

Location D - Sequential Body Number
The number assigned to that particular body at the assembly plant.

Location E - Interior Trim Code
775 - Black standard vinyl
776 - Dark Blue standard vinyl
777 - Sandalwood standard vinyl
778 - Dark Jade standard vinyl
779 - Dark Saddle standard vinyl
785 - Black custom cloth
786 - Dark Blue custom cloth
787 - Dark Jade custom cloth
789 - Black/White custom cloth
792 - Dark Saddle custom cloth

Location F - Lower Body Paint Code
The first number indicates lower body color.
11 - Antique White
13 - Nevada Silver
19 - Tuxedo Black
24 - Ascot Blue
26 - Mulsanne Blue
42 - Cottonwood Green
43 - Lime Green
49 - Antique Green
52 - Sunflower Yellow
53 - Placer Gold
61 - Sandalwood
62 - Burnt Orange
67 - Classic Copper
75 - Cranberry Red
78 - Rosewood Metallic

Location G - Upper Body Paint Code/Vinyl Top Code
A number here would designate no vinyl top. The number should match the lower body color number.
A - White
B - Black
C - Blue
F - Brown
G - Green

Location H - Build Date Code
01 - January
02 - February
03 - March
04 - April
05 - May
06 - June
07 - July
08 - August
09 - September
10 - October
11 - November
12 - December
A - 1st week of month
B - 2nd week of month
C - 3rd week of month
D - 4th week of month
E - 5th week of month

Location I - Option Code
If nothing is found here, the car is most probably a standard coupe. Not even RS option is indicated here. We have found this information on Norwood cars only.
Z28 - Z28 option
28.19 - Z28 with black stripes
Z27 - Super Sport
Z28.19 - Z28 with black stripes
28.10 - Z28 with white stripes
Z28.10 - Z28 with white stripes
LS3 - SS with 396/300hp Turbo-Jet

1971 Camaro Protect-O-Plate

```
                    123671N123456(A)      H(B)
F0302CGP(C)         CB0227G(D)            1(E)
P7B26(F)            1(G)1(H)4(I)3(H)4(K)5(L)1(M)
                                          (N)
                    Chevrolet Owner
                    123 Main St.
                    Anywhere, AB          3-15-71
                            USA
```

Location A - Vehicle Identification Number

12487 - Sport Coupe, V-8 engine
12387 - Sport Coupe, six-cylinder
N - Plant (Norwood)
L - Plant (Los Angeles)
123456 - Sequential Body Number

Location B - Carburetor Source

B - Bay City
C - Carter
H - Holley
R - Rochester

Location C - Engine Production Code

F - Flint
K - McKinnon Industries
S - Saginaw
T - Tonawanda
V - Flint Engine Plant
1-12 Month Production Code:
1 - January
2 - February
3 - March
4 - April
5 - May
6 - June
7 - July
8 - August
9 - September
10 - October
11 - November
12 - December
01-31 Day of Month
1971 Engine Codes:
250/145hp
CAA - Manual Transmission
CAB - Powerglide
307/200hp
CCA - Manual Transmission, Powerglide
CCC - Turbo Hydra-matic
350
CGB - 350/245 Powerglide

CGA - L65, four-speed, two-barrel carburetor
CGC - L65, Turbo Hydra-matic
CGK - L48, four-speed
CGL - L48, Turbo Hydra-matic
CJG - L48, four-speed
CJD - L48, Turbo Hydra-matic
CGP - 350/330 (Z28), four-speed
CGR - 350/330 (Z28) Turbo Hydra-matic
396
CLA - LS3, four-speed, four-barrel carburetor
CLB - LS3, Turbo Hydra-matic

Location D - Rear Axle Code

CA - 2.73 posi
CB - 4.10
CG - 3.73
CJ - 3.42 posi
CK - 3.42
GX - 3.08
GY - 3.08 posi
GZ - 2.73
01-12 Month Production Code:
01 - January
02 - February
03 - March
04 - April
05 - May
06 - June
07 - July
08 - August
09 - September
10 - October
11 - November
12 - December
01-31 Day of Month
Plant Codes:
B - Buffalo
G - Chevrolet Gear and Axle
K - McKinnon
W - Warren

Location E - Month of Vehicle Build

8 - August 1970
9 - September 1970
O - October 1970
N - November 1970
D - December 1970
1 - January 1971
2 - February 1971
3 - March 1971
4 - April 1971
5 - May 1971
6 - June 1971
7 - July 1971

All cars came with jacking instructions. Those with posi-traction rear option came with "CAUTION" decal explaining positraction system.

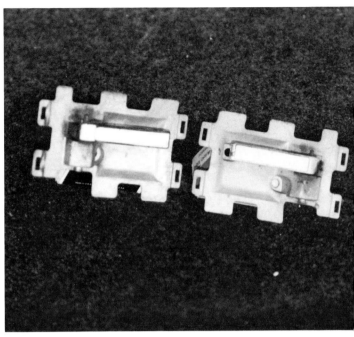

1970-71 deluxe inside door handles. 1970-73 standard interior and 1972-73 deluxe interior shared the same handle, which was different than 70-71 deluxe shown here.

Location F - Transmission Number
D - Saginaw three-speed OD
K - McKinnon Industries four-speed
C - Cleveland Powerglide
M - Muncie three-speed
R - Saginaw four-speed
T - Toledo Powerglide
K - McKinnon Industries three-speed
P - Muncie four-speed
E - McKinnon Industries Powerglide
H - Muncie Heavy-Duty
A - Cleveland Torque Drive
X - Cleveland THM 350
B - Cleveland THM 350
Y - Toledo THM 350
1 - Model Year (1971)
A-T Calendar Month:
A - January
B - February
C - March
D - April
E - May
H - June
K - July
M - August
P - September
R - October
S - November
T - December
01-31 Day of Month
Turbo Hydra-matic Code: Contains model year, model identification, and production date
71 - Year 1971
Build Date: Code of 1971 model year begins with

first day of the calendar year 1970 and continues through the 1970 calendar year.

Location G - Power Steering
1 - N40 Power Steering only

Location H - Power Brakes
1 - J50 Power Brakes

Location I - Radio Option
3 - U63 AM Radio
3 - U69 AM/FM

Location J - Disc Brake Option
3 - J52 Disc Brakes

Location K - Air Conditioning Option
1 - C60 Air Conditioning

Location L - Power Window Equipment Option
Power windows were not available on 1971 Camaros

Location M - Power Seat Option
Power seats were not available on 1971 Camaros

Location N - Chevrolet Bow tie Emblem

Chapter 6

1972 Camaro

1972 Manufacturer's suggested retail price (MSRP) for base model Camaros

Model Number	Description	MSRP
12387	six-cylinder Sport Coupe	$2,729.70
12487	eight-cylinder Sport Coupe	2,819.70

Note: Manufacturer's suggested retail price **(MSRP)** includes the factory D&H charge (including federal excise tax) and recommended dealer delivery and handling charge. This price does not include transportation charges, state and local taxes, or any accessories or optional equipment that may be ordered.

Camaro Standard Equipment

Protective inner skirts at both front and rear wheel openings; flush-and-dry rocker panels; energy-absorbing steering column; seat belts with pushbutton buckles for all passenger positions; passenger-guard door locks with deflecting lock buttons on all doors; four-way hazard flasher; dual master cylinder brake system with warning light and corrosion-resistant brake lines; latches on folding seat backs; dual-speed windshield wipers and washers; outside rearview mirror; back-up lights; side marker lights and parking lights that illuminate with headlights; padded instrument panel, sun visors, windshield pillars; reduced-glare instrument panel top, inside windshield moldings, horn button, steering hub, and windshield wiper arms and blades; inside day-night mirror with deflecting base; lane change feature in direction signal control; safety armrests; thick-laminate windshield; soft, low-profile window control knobs and coat hooks; energy-absorbing seat backs; yielding door and window control handles; energy-absorbing instrument panel with smooth contoured knobs and levers; tire safety rim; safety door latches and hinges; uniform shift quadrant; energy-absorbing steering wheel; snag-resistant steering wheel hardware; fuel tank and filler pipe security; high-level ventilation system; built-in blended-air heater and defroster system; Magic-Mirror acrylic lacquer finish; curved solid tempered plate glass windows; two-key lock system; weather-shielded key locks; color-keyed interior trim; scuff-resistant plastic cowl side panels with molded-in ventilator grilles; quality interior features and appointments; full-view instrument panel with instruments and controls; and locking glove compartment.

Consult authorized Chevrolet Dealers or your Fleet Representative for information on accessories and extra cost of optional equipment not listed.

General Motors Corporation reserves the right to make changes at any time, without notice, in prices, colors, materials, equipment, accessories, specifications, and models, and to discontinue models.

Body Structure

All-welded, heavy-gauge steel body
Double panel doors, hood, and deck lid
Counter-balanced hood and deck lid
Front and rear inner fenders for improved corrosion protection
Side-guard beam door structure
Cargo-guard all-steel luggage compartment bulkhead
Flush-and-dry rocker panels
Double panel roof

Body Insulation

Double-cushioned rubber body mounts
Rubber-cushioned front sheet metal
Jute pad floor insulation
Roof rear quarter area mastic insulation
Fibrous blanket cowl kick panel insulation
Asphalt-impregnated board rear seat back insulation

Body Sealing

Windshield and rear window bonded to body for positive sealing
Formed rubber deck lid seal
Weather-tight solid rubber window sill seals

Body Features

Thick-laminate windshield
Dual-speed electric windshield wipers and windshield washers
High-level ventilation system
Built-in blended-air heater and defroster system
Magic-Mirror acrylic lacquer finish
Curved solid tempered plate glass side and rear windows
Two-key lock system with keyless locking of all doors
Weather-shielded key locks
Scuff-resistant plastic cowl side panels
Astro-Ventilation system and full door-glass styling

Serial Numbers and Identification

Vehicle Identification Number (VIN)

Example: 1Q87H2N100037
1 - Make (1 for Chevrolet)
Q - Car Line and Series (Q for Camaro)
87 - Body Style (last two digits of model number)
H - Engine Type
D - 250/110 L6
F - 307/130 V-8
H - 350/165 V-8
K - 350/200 V-8
T - 350/255 V-8
U - 402/240 (396)
2 - Model Year (1972)
N - Assembly Plant
L - Van Nuys
N - Norwood
100037 - Sequential Body Number
Starting unit number is 100001 and up at each plant regardless of series.
Location: The vehicle identification number (VIN) is stamped on the plate attached to the top left-hand of the instrument panel.

Transmission Identification

Example: WJS2R13
WJ - Type Designation
S - Source Designation
R3 - three-speed, L6 and V-8 engines
R4 - three-speed, V-8
S - Muncie
WJ - four-speed, V-8 engine
R - Muncie
RB - Powerglide, L6 engine
RK - Powerglide, V-8 engine
C - Cleveland
B - Cleveland
SB - Turbo Hydra-matic, V-8 engine
CY - Turbo Hydra-matic, V-8 engine
B - Cleveland
Y - Toledo
— - Ypsilanti

Location:

Three-speed: stamped on left side just below cover.
Four-speed: stamped on right side of case at adapter.
Powerglide, Turbo Hydra-matic (Chevrolet): stamp-ed on right-hand side of pan.
Turbo Hydra-matic: nameplate tag on right-hand side of case.

Month
A - January
B - February
C - March
D - April
E - May
H - June
K - July
M - August
P - September
R - October
S - November
T - December
The letter D or N following the date indicates day or night shift

Engine Identification

Example: F1013CKT
F - Source Designation (Flint)
1013 - Production Month and Date
CKT - Type Designation
250ci six-cylinder
CBG - Regular engine, three-speed
CBJ - Regular engine, Powerglide

307ci eight-cylinder

CKG - Regular engine, three-speed
CKH - Regular engine, Powerglide
CKH - Regular engine, Turbo Hydra-matic (Chevrolet)

350ci eight-cylinder (RPO L65)
CKA - Optional engine, four-speed, two-barrel carburetor
CKB - Optional engine, Turbo Hydra-matic (Chevrolet)

350ci eight-cylinder (RPO L48)
CKK - Optional engine, four-speed, four-barrel carburetor
CKD - Optional engine, Turbo Hydra-matic (Chevrolet)

350ci eight-cylinder (RPO Z28)
CKS - Optional engine, four-speed, four-barrel carburetor
CKT - Optional engine, Turbo Hydra-matic (Chevrolet)

402ci (SS 396) eight-cylinder (RPO L34)
CLA - Optional engine, four-speed, four-barrel carburetor
CLB - Optional engine, Turbo Hydra-matic

Location:
Six-cylinder engine is stamped on pad on right side of cylinder block to rear of distributor.
Eight-cylinder engine is stamped on pad at front right side of cylinder block.

Month and Date
01 - January
02 - February
03 - March
04 - April
05 - May
06 - June
07 - July
08 - August
09 - September
10 - October
11 - November
12 - December

Rear Axle Identification
Identification number is stamped on bottom left or right of axle tube adjacent to carrier housing.

1972 Camaro Standard Equipment—

Exterior
Base Model
Header panel nameplate "C" and "Camaro"
Valance mounted parking lamp with clear lens and amber bulb
Single "Power Beam" headlamps
Bright headlamp bezel
Argent-colored one-piece radiator grille
Bright radiator grille outline molding
One-piece front bumper with dual bumper guards
License plate mounting provision in front center
Bright top and side windshield reveal molding
Two-speed windshield wipers and washers
Non-depressed park, dull-chrome wiper arms and 16" blades
Front marker lamps with amber lens - no bezel
Rear marker lamps with red lens - no bezel
Engine displacement numerals on fender (only with 350 or 396 engines)
Front fender "Camaro" nameplate
Rectangular left-hand rearview mirror
Bright chrome flush door handles
Bright wide rocker panel molding - bright
Bright lower window sealing strip bead
Bright body lock pillar vertical seal retainer
Hubcaps
Deck lid "Camaro by Chevrolet" nameplate
Bright rear window reveal moldings
Dual rear end panel mounted taillamps and back-up lamps with bright outer bezel

Style Trim (RPO Z21)
Header panel nameplate "C" and "Camaro"
Valance mounted parking lamp with clear lens and amber bulb
Single "Power Beam" headlamps
Bright headlamp bezel
Argent-colored one-piece radiator grille
Bright radiator grille outline molding
One-piece front bumper with dual bumper guards
License plate mounting provision in front center
Bright top and side windshield reveal molding
Two-speed windshield wipers and washers
Non-depressed park, dull-chrome wiper arms and 16" blades
Bright hood and fender rear edge molding
Front marker lamps with amber lens - no bezel
Rear marker lamps with red lens - no bezel
Engine displacement numerals on fender (only with 350 or 396 engines)
Front fender "Camaro" nameplate
Rectangular left-hand rearview mirror
Body colored tape insert on flush door handles
Bright wide rocker panel molding
Bright body lock pillar vertical seal retainer

Bright roof drip moldings
Bright door belt reveal molding
Hubcaps
Deck lid "Camaro by Chevrolet" nameplate
Bright rear window reveal moldings
Dual rear end panel mounted taillamps and back-up lamps with bright outer bezel
Rear bumper face bar to body filler

Rally Sport (RPO Z22)
Header panel nameplate "C" and "Camaro"
Special parking lamp adjacent to headlamp with bright bezel and ornament
Single "Power Beam" headlamps
Bright headlamp bezel
Special two-piece, black-painted radiator grille with argent-painted leading edges
Bright radiator grille filler
Individual right-hand and left-hand front bumpers
Resilient grille frame with rubber-protected center grille section of bumper stock
License plate mounting provision at front right bumper
Bright top and side windshield reveal molding
Two-speed windshield wipers and washers
Concealed black chrome-finished wiper - articulated left blade and 18" wiper blades
Front marker lamps with amber lens - no bezel
Rear marker lamps with red lens - no bezel
Engine displacement numerals on fender (only with 350 or 396 engines)
Rally Sport fender nameplates
Rectangular left-hand rearview mirror
Bright chrome flush door handles
Bright wide rocker panel molding
Bright lower window sealing strip bead
Bright body lock pillar vertical seal retainer
Hubcaps
Deck lid "Camaro by Chevrolet" nameplate
Bright rear window reveal moldings
Dual rear end panel mounted taillamps and back-up lamps with bright outer bezel

Super Sport (RPO Z27)
Header panel nameplate "C" and "Camaro"
Valance mounted parking lamp with clear lens and amber bulb
Single "Power Beam" headlamps
Bright headlamp bezel
Black painted radiator grille
Bright radiator grille outline molding
Radiator grille "SS" emblem
One-piece front bumper with dual bumper guards
License plate mounting provision in front center

Bright top and side windshield reveal molding
Two-speed windshield wipers and washers
Concealed black chrome-finished wipers - articulated left blade and 18" Wiper blades
Front marker lamps with amber lens - no bezel
Rear marker lamps with red lens - no bezel
Engine displacement numerals on fender (only with 350 or 396 engines)
"SS" front fender emblems
Rectangular left-hand rearview mirror
Bright chrome flush door handles
Bright wide rocker panel molding
Bright lower window sealing strip bead
Bright body lock pillar vertical seal retainer
White lettered wide oval 14" tires on 14"x7" wheels
Hubcaps
Deck lid "Camaro by Chevrolet" nameplate
Bright rear window reveal moldings
Dual rear end panel mounted taillamps and back-up lamps with bright outer bezel
Black painted rear end panel (SS 396 only)
Chrome-plated tailpipe ends - dual

Z28 (RPO Z28)
Header panel nameplate "C" and "Camaro"
Valance mounted parking lamp with clear lens and amber bulb
Single "Power Beam" headlamps
Bright headlamp bezel
Black painted radiator grille
Bright radiator grille outline molding
Radiator grille Z28 emblem
One-piece front bumper with dual bumper guards
License plate mounting provision in front center
Wide hood paint stripes
Bright top and side windshield reveal molding
Two-speed windshield wipers and washers
Non-depressed park, dull-chrome wiper arms and 16" blades
Front marker lamps with amber lens - no bezel
Rear marker lamps with red lens - no bezel
Z28 front fender nameplates
Rectangular left-hand rearview mirror
Bright chrome flush door handles
Bright wide rocker panel molding
Bright lower window sealing strip bead
Bright body lock pillar vertical seal retainer
White lettered wide oval 15" tires on special 15"x7" wheels
Deck lid "Camaro by Chevrolet" nameplate
Bright rear window reveal moldings
Dual rear end panel mounted taillamps and back-up lamps with bright outer bezel
Z28 identification on spoiler

Deck lid spoiler
Wide paint stripes on deck lid and spoiler
Rear bumper guards
Chrome-plated tailpipe ends - dual

1972 Camaro Standard Equipment— Interior
Base Model
Trim color instrument panel pad
Bright accented black instrument cluster
Glove compartment door lock
"Camaro" glove compartment nameplate
Bright side kick-pad ventilation control knob
Bright Astro-ventilation control knob
T-handle parking brake release
Instrument panel Astro-ventilation outlets
Windshield wiper and washer switch (slide-type, depress to wash)
Lighting control knob - black soft vinyl with symbol
Speedometer, odometer, and fuel gauge
Temperature, generator, oil pressure, and brake warning telltale lights
"Fasten Seat Belt" lamp in instrument panel (effective 1-1-72)
Hi-beam and turn signal indicators
Automatic shift quadrant cover plate
Clock hole cover
Radio hole cover
Ashtray
Cigarette lighter knob - black soft vinyl with symbol
Blended-air heater with illuminated control plate
Black steering column
Soft black vinyl four-spoke steering wheel
Soft black vinyl center horn button with bow tie emblem
Steering column ignition switch with integral steering wheel and transmission lock
Black plastic hazard flasher knob
Soft black turn signal knob
One low-note horn
Premier vinyl-coated perforated headlining
Trim color windshield header, pillar, roof side rails, and rear window moldings
Black ten-inch prismatic rearview mirror with black padded edges
Black rearview mirror support - windshield mounted
Padded sunshades
Trim-colored plastic coat hooks
Center dome lamp with bright bezel
Door jamb dome lamp switches
Black front seat shoulder belt anchor covers
Front seat shoulder belt retention

Color-keyed plastic hook and clear plastic hanger
Full foam bucket front seats with integral head restraints
Rear seat - dual cushions with single, full-width back rest, cotton padded
Black front seat adjuster handle
Black front bucket seat back latch
Passenger compartment floor carpet
Luggage compartment spatter paint
Front and rear seat belts: four; Base: Black with black plastic mini-buckles, locking retractors (Note: For start of production, seat belts were carried over from 1971 model year. Seat belts represented here are 1972 interim changes to meet motor vehicle safety requirements.)
Front shoulder belts: two; Base: Black with "D" ring attachment; stowage by plastic trim color trough (see note above)
Trim color seat back hinge arm cover
Injection molded lower door trim panel incorporating built-in padded armrest, front and rear map pockets, and coin receptacle
Built-in rear quarter panel armrest
Clear plastic window control handle knobs
Bright door lock buttons
Vinyl and plastic door and plastic quarter trim
Recessed door handle
Trim colored plastic inside door handle cup
Soft black transmission shift level knob with white shift pattern
Floor-mounted transmission shift lever

Special Interior Group (RPO Z23)
Trim color instrument panel pad
Woodgrain appliqué on instrument cluster
Glove compartment door lock
"Camaro" glove compartment nameplate
Bright side kick-pad ventilation control knob
Bright Astro-ventilation control knob
T-handle parking brake release
Instrument panel Astro-ventilation outlets
Windshield wiper and washer switch (slide-type, depress to wash)
Lighting control knob - black soft vinyl with symbol
Speedometer, odometer, and fuel gauge
Temperature, generator, oil pressure, and brake warning telltale lights
"Fasten Seat Belt" lamp in instrument panel (effective 1-1-72)
Hi-beam and turn signal indicators
Automatic shift quadrant cover plate
Clock hole cover
Radio hole cover

Dual-snorkel air cleaner on 1970-72 Camaros.

Ashtray
Cigarette lighter knob - black soft vinyl with symbol
Blended-air heater with illuminated control plate
Black steering column
Soft black vinyl four-spoke steering wheel
Soft black vinyl center horn button with bow tie emblem
Steering column ignition switch with integral steering wheel and transmission lock
Black plastic hazard flasher knob
Soft black turn signal knob
One low-note horn
Additional instrument cluster lighting
Premier vinyl-coated perforated headlining
Trim color windshield header, pillar, roof side rails, and rear window moldings
Black ten-inch prismatic rearview mirror with black padded edges
Black rearview mirror support - windshield mounted
Padded sunshades
Trim-colored plastic coat hooks
Center dome lamp with bright bezel
Door jamb dome lamp switches
Black front seat shoulder belt anchor covers
Front seat shoulder belt retention
Color-keyed plastic hook and clear plastic hanger
Full foam bucket front seats with integral head restraints
Rear seat - dual cushions with single, full-width back rest, cotton padded
Black front seat adjuster handle
Black front bucket seat back latch
Passenger compartment floor carpet
Luggage compartment spatter paint

Front and rear seat belts: four; Base: Black with black plastic mini-buckles, locking retractors (Note: For start of production, seat belts were carried over from 1971 model year. Seat belts represented here are 1972 interim changes to meet motor vehicle safety requirements.)

Front shoulder belts: two; Base: Black with "D" ring attachment; stowage by plastic trim color trough (see note above)

Trim color seat back hinge arm cover

Injection molded lower door trim panel incorporating built-in padded armrest, front and rear map pockets, and coin receptacle

Built-in rear quarter panel armrests

Clear plastic window control handle knobs

Bright door lock buttons

Vinyl and plastic door and plastic quarter trim

Recessed door handles

Trim colored plastic inside door handle cup

Soft black transmission shift level knob with white shift pattern

Floor-mounted transmission shift lever

Custom interior (RPO Z87)

Trim color instrument panel pad

Woodgrain appliqué instrument cluster

Glove compartment door lock

"Camaro" glove compartment nameplate

Bright side kick-pad ventilation control knob

Bright Astro-ventilation control knob

T-handle parking brake release

Instrument panel Astro-ventilation outlets

Windshield wiper and washer switch (slide-type, depress to wash)

Lighting control knob - black soft vinyl with symbol

Speedometer, odometer, and fuel gauge

Temperature, generator, oil pressure, and brake warning telltale lights

"Fasten Seat Belt" lamp in instrument panel (effective 1-1-72)

Hi-beam and turn signal indicators

Glove compartment lamp

Automatic shift quadrant cover plate

Clock hole cover

Radio hole cover

Ashtray

Cigarette lighter knob - black soft vinyl with symbol

Blended-air heater with illuminated control plate

Black steering column

Soft black vinyl four-spoke steering wheel

Soft black vinyl center horn button with bow tie emblem

Steering column ignition switch with integral steering wheel and transmission lock

Black plastic hazard flasher knob

Soft black turn signal knob

Argent-finish accent beads on lower instrument panel

One low-note horn

Additional instrument cluster lighting

Premier vinyl-coated perforated headlining

Trim color windshield header, pillar, roof side rails, and rear window moldings

Black ten-inch prismatic rearview mirror with black padded edges

Black rearview mirror support - windshield mounted

Padded sunshades

Trim-colored plastic coat hooks

Center dome lamp with bright bezel

Door jamb dome lamp switches

Black front seat shoulder belt anchor covers

Front seat shoulder belt retention

Color-keyed plastic hook and clear plastic hanger

Full foam bucket front seats with integral head restraints

Deluxe seat trim

Rear seat - dual cushions with single, full-width back rest, cotton padded

Black front seat adjuster handle

Black front bucket seat back latch

Passenger compartment floor carpet

Luggage compartment rubber floor mat

Front and rear seat belts: four; Base: Black with black plastic mini-buckles, locking retractors (Note: For start of production, seat belts were carried over from 1971 model year. Seat belts represented here are 1972 interim changes to meet motor vehicle safety requirements)

Optional front and rear seat belts: Color-coordinated belts with plastic color-keyed mini-buckles and locking retractors

Front shoulder belts: two; Base: Black with "D" ring attachment; stowage by plastic trim color trough (see note above)

Optional front shoulder belts: two; Color-coordinated, "D" ring attachment; stowage by plastic trim color trough

Trim color seat back hinge arm cover

Injection molded lower door trim panel incorporating built-in padded armrest, front and rear map pockets, and coin receptacle

Built-in rear quarter panel armrest

Clear plastic window control handle knobs

Bright door lock buttons

Vinyl and plastic door and plastic quarter trim

Woodgrain insert on door trim panel with bright edges
Recessed door handles
Chrome inside door handle cup with black painted insert
Additional body insulation
Full molded hood insulation
Soft black transmission shift level knob with white shift pattern
Floor-mounted transmission shift lever

New Features for 1972
New vinyl roof color choices
New interior color choices
Fifteen Magic-Mirror acrylic colors (ten new)
New standard vinyl steering wheel
Bolder, large grid pattern on standard grille
New hood latch

Occupant Protection Features
Seat belts with pushbutton buckles for all passenger positions
Shoulder belts with pushbutton buckles - driver and right front passenger
Two front seat head restraints
Energy-absorbing steering column
Passenger-guard door locks with forward mounted lock buttons
Safety door latches and hinges
Folding seat back latches
Energy-absorbing padded instrument panel and front seat back tops
Contoured full roof inner panel or windshield header
Thick-laminate windshield
Padded sun visors
Safety armrests
Safety steering wheel
Side-guard beams
Cargo-guard luggage compartment
Full tank impact security
Glove compartment and console door latch impact security
Yielding windshield pillar moldings
Smooth-contoured door and window regulator handles
Soft, low profile window control knobs, coat hooks, and dome light
Stamped steel door hinges
High-strength front seat anchorages and construction
High-strength rear seat retention

Accident Prevention Features
Side marker lights and reflectors (front side marker lights flash with directional signal)
Parking lights that illuminate with headlights
Four-way hazard warning flasher
Back-up lights
Lane-change feature in direction signal control
Windshield defroster, washers, and dual-speed wipers
Wide-view inside day-night mirror (vinyl-edged, shatter-resistant glass) and deflecting support
Outside rearview mirror
Dual-action safety hood latches
Dual master cylinder brake system with warning light
Headlight aiming access provision
Low-glare instrument panel top, inside windshield moldings, wiper arms and blades, and steering wheel metallic surfaced
Safety wheel rims
Uniform shift quadrant
No winged wheel nuts, discs, and caps
Self-adjusting brakes

Anti-Theft Features
Anti-theft ignition key warning buzzer
Anti-theft steering column lock
Multiple key combinations
Visible vehicle identification
Tamper-resistant odometer with telltale feature

Traditional Quality Features
Astro-Ventilation system with large rectangular vent ports on instrument panel
Side marker lights front and rear
Long hood styling
Slender full-width front bumper, silver-finish grille in large grid pattern, license plate mounting centered between front bumper guards, wide parking lights below bumper
Single-unit "Power Beam" headlights recessed in bright frames on front fenders
Wide body sill moldings
Flush mounted door handles
Recessed door handles
Swept-back roof and rear deck styling
Strato-bucket seats standard equipment
Wide (ten-inch) inside day-night rearview mirror
Outer front seat belt retractors
Acoustically engineered double-panel roof structure
Forward-mounted door lock buttons
Magic-Mirror acrylic lacquer finish

Flush-and-dry rocker panels
Curved side windows
Flush-mounted windshield and rear window bonded to body
Dual-speed electric windshield wipers
Built-in blended-air heater and defroster system
Inner fenders front and rear
108" wheelbase
Foot-operated parking brake
Deep-twist carpet floor covering
Suspended accelerator pedal
Efficient valve-in-head design
Positive-shift starter
Quiet hydraulic valve lifters
Sealed side-terminal Energizer battery
Automatic choke on all engines
Advanced accessory drive system on all V-8 engines
Delcotron generator
Seven main bearing six-cylinder engine with fully counterweighted crankshaft
Transmission-controlled spark advance
Separate front frame unit
Advanced design front suspension with forward mounted steering linkage
Wide front and rear tread
Bias belted ply tires
Bias-mounted rear shock absorbers (curb side unit mounted ahead of axle, other mounted behind) for excellent suspension control
Computer-selected front and rear springs
Independent coil front suspension
Multi-leaf rear springs
Disc brakes standard on front wheels (power operation optional)
Finned rear brake drums
Self-adjusting brakes
Precise ball-race steering

1972 Camaro Options and Accessories
When Factory Installed
V-8 Models (130hp Turbo-Fire 307 V-8)
12487 Sport Coupe $2,819.70
Six-cylinder Models (110hp Turbo-Thrift 250 Six)
12387 Sport Coupe   2,729.70

Z27
Camaro SS: Includes 200hp Turbo-Fire 350 V-8 engine with bright accents; heavy-duty engine mounts and starter; dual exhausts; power brakes; left-hand remote control mirror; special hood insulation; F70-14B bias belted ply white letter tires; 14"x7" wheels; black finished grille; Hide-A-Way windshield wipers; and "SS" emblems on

steering wheel, grille, and front fenders V-8 models with four-speed or Turbo Hydra-matic transmission only) $306.35
In California $280.35

LS3
240hp Turbo-Fire 396ci V-8 engine (available only with Camaro SS package; includes sport suspension and black-finished rear panel; not available in California) $96.00

Z87
Custom interior: includes deluxe seat and sidewall trim; cloth seats; glove compartment light and additional instrument cluster lighting; wood-grained accents on instrument cluster; steering wheel and door trim pads; luggage compartment mat plus special engine compartment, hood, and interior insulation $113.00

Z23
Accent Group Interior: includes glove compartment light, additional instrument cluster lighting, wood-grained accents on instrument cluster and steering wheel (included with Custom interior) $21.00

Z22
Rally Sport: includes special black finished grille with special rubber tipped vertical center bar and resilient body color grille frame; independent left-hand and right-hand front bumpers replacing full-width bumper; license plate bracket mounted below right-hand bumper; parking lights with bright accents mounted on grille panel; Hide-A-Way windshield wipers; RS emblems on steering wheel and Rally Sport front fender nameplates (Rally Sport emblems deleted with Camaro SS or Z28 Special Performance Package) $118.00

Z21
Style Trim: includes bright roof drip, window, hood panel, and belt moldings plus bright accented parking lights, taillights, and back-up lights $56.00

Z28
Special Performance Package: includes 255hp Turbo-Fire special 350ci V-8 with finned aluminum rocker covers and bright accents; left-hand remote control and right-hand manual control sport mirrors; special instrumentation; power brakes; 3.73:1 ratio posi-traction rear axle, dual exhausts; black finished grille; Z28 emblems on

grille and front fenders; rear bumper guards; sport suspension; heavy-duty engine mounts, starter, radiator, and front and rear springs; 15"x7" wheels with bright lug nuts, special center caps, and trim rings; F60-15B bias belted ply white letter tires; Z28 decal on rear panel; special paint stripes on hood and rear deck (V-8 model with four-speed or Turbo Hydra-matic transmission only; not available with air conditioning, wheel covers, or rally wheels) $769.15
In California $743.15

Feature Groups

ZP5 Appearance Guard Group includes

B93	Door Edge Guards	6.00
B37	Color Keyed Front and Rear Floor Mats	12.00
D34	Vanity Visor Mirror	3.00

ZJ9   Auxiliary Lighting: includes ashtray, courtesy, luggage compartment, under-hood, and glove compartment lights   17.50
              with Custom interior Group   15.00

Power Teams

Engines: See Power Team chart for complete engine specifications, model, and transmission availability.

L65   165hp Turbo-Fire V-8 engine   26.00

Transmissions: See Power Team chart for availability

M35   Powerglide automatic with:
              six-cylinder base engine   174.00
              eight-cylinder base engine   185.00
M40   Turbo Hydra-matic automatic with base V-8 engine   210.00
              with 240hp Camaro SS engine   231.00
              with Z28 Special Performance Package   297.00
M20   Four-speed wide range (for use with optional engines only)   200.00
M21   Four-speed close ratio (available only with 240hp Camaro SS or Z28 Special Performance Package)   200.00
M22   Heavy-Duty four-speed close ratio (available only with Z28 Special Performance Package)   231.00
G80   Posi-traction rear axle   45.00

Axle Ratios:

YD1   Special axle ratio for trailering (available only with 130hp or 240hp engine and Turbo Hydra-matic transmission)   12.00
ZQ9   Performance axle ratio (available only with Z28)   12.00

Console on 1970-72 Camaros.

Power Assists

J50   Power Brakes (included with Camaro SS or Z28 Special Performance Package)   46.00
N40   Power Steering, variable ratio   130.00

Other Options

C50   Rear Window Defroster   31.00
C60   Air Conditioning, Four Season: includes heavy-duty radiator and 61-amp generator (V-8 models only; not available with Z28 Special Performance Package)   397.00
D80   Spoiler, Front and Rear: includes front valance spoiler, rear deck, and rear side panel spoiler; front spoiler shipped loose for dealer installation   77.00
T60   Battery, Heavy-Duty: 15-plate, 80 amp-hr   15.00
AK1   Custom Deluxe Seat and Shoulder Belts: includes five seat and two front shoulder, brushed metal buckles, and color keyed belts (replaces standard belts which were black)   14.50
AN6   Adjustable Seat Back, two positions (driver's side only)   18.00
A01   Soft-Ray Tinted Glass, all windows   39.00
A02   Soft-Ray Tinted Windshield   19.00
D55   Console: includes floor-mounted shift lever (when automatic transmission is ordered), rear seat courtesy light, compartment and ashtray   57.00
U14   Special Instrumentation: includes tachometer, ammeter, and temperature gauges plus electric clock mounted in instrument panel cluster, and additional instrument cluster lighting (V-8 models only; included with Z28 Special

Performance Package) 82.00

U35   Electric Clock (included with special instrumentation or Z28 Special Performance Package) 16.00

U63   AM Radio 65.00

U69   AM/FM Radio 135.00

U80   Rear Seat Speaker 15.00

C08   Vinyl Roof Cover, includes bright roof drip molding (AA - White BB - Black FF - Tan GG - Green TT - Convertible) 87.00

N33   Comfortilt Steering Wheel 44.00

NK4   Sport Steering Wheel 15.00

F41   Special Suspension: includes special front stabilizer, rear stabilizer and special front and rear shock absorbers (V-8 models with F70-14 tires only; included with 240hp Turbo-Jet 396 Camaro SS engine or Z28 Special Performance Package) 30.00

YF5   Emission Test: to conform with California registration requirements (not available with 130hp or 240hp engines) 15.00

C24   Hide-A-Way Windshield Wipers, includes articulated left-hand blades (included with Rally Sport or Camaro SS) 21.00

D35   Exterior Sport Mirror: left-hand remote control (included with Camaro SS or Z28 Special Performance Package) 15.00

VF3   Deluxe Front and Rear Bumpers: includes slender black resilient front and rear bumper cushions and rear bumper guards 36.00
with Z28 Special Performance Package 24.00

V01   Heavy-Duty Radiator (V-8 models only; included with air conditioning or Z28 Special Performance Package) 14.00

PL3   Tires, E78-14B bias belted ply white stripe (not available with Camaro SS) 28.00

PL4   Tires, F70-14B bias belted ply white letter, includes 14"x7" wheels (V-8 models only; included with Camaro SS) 82.85

PY4   Tires, F70-14B bias belted ply white stripe, includes 14"x7" wheels (V-8 models only; no charge with Camaro SS) 69.85

PM7   Tires, F60-15B glass belted whitewall tires

P01   Wheel Covers, bright metal (not available with Z28 Special Performance Package) 26.00

P02   Wheel Covers, custom (not available with Z28 Special Performance Package) 82.00

ZJ7   Rally Wheels, includes special 14"x7" wheels, hub- caps, and trim rings (not available with E78-14 tires) 44.00

Dealer-Installed Custom Features and Accessories

Description	Part No.
Radio Antenna, AM, and AM/FM Front	994128
Power Brakes	993989
Locking Gas Cap	994171
GM Infant Safety Carrier	994259
Vinyl Side Molding, universal, 38 ft. roll	994227
Rear Deck Lid Luggage Carrier	993862
Auto Compass	993915
Litter Container, Saddle-type	
Black	986607
Blue	986602
Fawn	986603
Red	986608
Wheel Covers, 14"	994138
Wheel Covers, 14" Coolie-Hat	993815
Wire Wheel Covers, 14"	994206
Combination Tissue Dispenser and Litter Container	993920
Rear Window Defogger	994182
Rear Bumper Guards	993972
Door Edge Guards	993964
Fender Guards, front or rear, pair	993985
Fire Extinguisher	994177
Fire Extinguisher Recharge Kit	985593
Highway Emergency Kit	993537
Trailer Wiring Harness	993589
Frame Mounted Trailer Hitch	994170
Engine Block Heater, except 396 and 454	994161
Engine Block Heater, with 396 and 454	994162
Radiator Hose Heater, 1.5-inch diameter hose	994186
Lights	
Ashtray	994008
Glove Compartment	993982
Luggage Compartment	993997
Under-hood	994234
Hood Pin Locks with key	994203
Contour Floor Mats	
Black, front	994247
Black, rear	994248
Dark Blue, front	994235
Dark Blue, rear	994241
Convertible, front	994236
Convertible, rear	994242
Dark Green, front	994239
Dark Green, rear	994245
Right-hand Rearview Mirror	994039
Right-hand Sport Mirror	994226
Trailering Mirror	994038
Vanity Visor Mirror	993723
AM/FM Stereo Radio/Tape Player Combination	994113

Nice view of a standard 70-73 Z28 with full-width front bumper and one-piece grill.

AM Radio/Tape Player Combination	994112
AM/FM Pushbutton Radio	994110
AM/FM Stereo Radio	994111
AM Pushbutton Radio	994109
AM Radio/Tape Combination Replacement	994096
AM/FM Stereo Radio/Tape Combination Replacement	994097
Rear Speakers	994121
Hand-Portable Spotlight	987112
Seat Belt Buckle Retainers	994000
In Car Air Heater	992264
Battery Blanket	992191
Demountable Ski Rack, rain-gutter type	993782

1972 Camaro Trim Plate

```
ST 72 (A) 12487 (B)     NOR (C)    171489 BDY (D)

TR 777 (E)              53 (F) -53(G)        PNT

04E (H)   A51(I)      Z27 (J)    ZR8 (K)
```

Location A - Model Year
72 - 1972

Location B - Body Style
12487 - Sport Coupe

Location C - Assembly Plant
NOR - Norwood, Ohio
BL - Van Nuys, California

Location D - Sequential Body Number
The number assigned to that particular body at the assembly plant.

Location E - Interior Trim Code
775 - Black standard vinyl
776 - Dark Blue standard vinyl
777 - Dark Green standard vinyl
778 - Medium Tan standard vinyl
779 - Convertible Tan standard vinyl
780 - White standard vinyl
785 - Black custom cloth
786 - Dark Blue/Black custom cloth
787 - Dark Green/Black custom cloth
788 - Convertible Tan/Black custom cloth

Location F - Lower Body Paint Code
The first number indicates lower body color.
11 - Antique White
14 - Pewter Silver

24 - Ascot Blue
26 - Mulsanne Blue
36 - Spring Green
43 - Gulf Green
48 - Sequoia Green
50 - Convertible Tan
53 - Placer Gold
56 - Cream Yellow
57 - Golden Brown
63 - Mohave Gold
65 - Orange Flame
68 - Midnight Bronze
75 - Cranberry Red

Location G - Upper Body Paint Code/Vinyl Top Code
A number here would designate no vinyl top. The number should match the lower body color number.
A - White
G - Green
B - Black
T - Convertible Tan
F - Tan

Location H - Build Date Code
01 - January
02 - February
03 - March
04 - April
05 - May
06 - June
07 - July
08 - August
09 - September
10 - October
11 - November
12 - December
A - 1st week of month
B - 2nd week of month
C - 3rd week of month
D - 4th week of month
E - 5th week of month

Location I - Seat Style
A51 in this position indicates Strato-Back Front Bucket Seats

Location J - Option Code
No markings here indicate a six-cylinder coupe or basic small block V-8 (Norwood cars only).
Z28 - RPO Z28
Z27 - RPO Z27 Super Sport

Location K - Z28 Stripe Color

ZR8 - White hood and deck striping - Norwood cars only

YF8 - Black hood and deck striping - Norwood cars only

1972 Camaro Protect-O-Plate

```
                1Q87H2N123456(A)      H(B)
F0302CKS(C)     CB0227G(D)            1(E)
P2B26(F)        1(G)1(H)4(I)3(J)4(K)5(L)1(M)
                                      (N)
                Chevrolet Owner
                123 Main St.
                Anywhere, AB        3-15-72
                        USA
```

Location A - Vehicle Identification Number

1 - Chevrolet
Q - Camaro
87 - Last two digits of body style
H - Engine Code
        D - 250 L6
        F - 307 V-8
        H - 350, two-barrel
        K - 350 RPO Z27
        T - 350 RPO Z28
        U - 396 V-8
N - Plant
        L - Los Angeles
        N - Norwood
123456 - Sequential Body Number

Location B - Carburetor Source

B - Bay City
C - Carter
H - Holley
R - Rochester

Location C - Engine Production Code

F - Flint
K - McKinnon Industries
S - Saginaw
T - Tonawanda
V - Flint Engine Plant
1-12 Month Production Code:
1 - January
2 - February
3 - March
4 - April
5 - May
6 - June
7 - July
8 - August
9 - September
10 - October
11 - November
12 - December

01-31 Day of Month 1972 Engine Codes:
250/110hp
CBG - Manual Transmission
CBJ - Powerglide
CDM - Manual Transmission with A.I.R.
CDL - Powerglide with A.I.R.
CBA - Manual Transmission with Exhaust Emission Control
CSD - Powerglide with Exhaust Emission Control

307/130hp
CKG - Manual Transmission
CKH - Powerglide
CTK - Turbo Hydra-matic
CAY - Manual Transmission with Exhaust Emission Control
CAZ - Powerglide or THM with Exhaust Emission Control
CMA - Turbo Hydra-matic with Exhaust Emission Control

350
CKA - Manual Transmission (L65)
CTL - Turbo Hydra-matic (L65)
CRG - Manual Transmission with A.I.R. (L65)
CRD - Turbo Hydra-matic with A.I.R. (L65)
CKK - Manual Transmission (L48)
CKD - Turbo Hydra-matic (L48)
CMH - Manual Transmission with EEC (L65)
CMD - Turbo Hydra-matic with EEC (L65)
CDG - Manual Transmission with EEC (L48)
CDD - Turbo Hydra-matic with EEC (L48)
CKS - Manual Transmission (Z28)
CKT - Turbo Hydra-matic (Z28)

396
CLA - Manual Transmission
CLB - Turbo Hydra-matic
CTA - Manual Transmission with A.I.R.
CTB - Turbo Hydra-matic with A.I.R.

The same Z28 fender emblem was used on all 1970-73 Z28 Camaros.

Location D - Rear Axle Code
CA - 2.73 posi
CB - 4.10
CG - 3.73
CJ - 3.42 posi
CK - 3.42
GX - 3.08
GY - 3.08 posi
GZ - 2.73
01-12 Month
01 - January
02 - February
03 - March
04 - April
05 - May
06 - June
07 - July
08 - August
09 - September
10 - October
11 - November
12 - December
01-31 Day of Month
Plant Codes:
B - Buffalo
G - Chevrolet Gear and Axle
K - McKinnon
W - Warren

Location E - Month of Vehicle Build
8 - August 1971
9 - September 1971
O - October 1971
N - November 1971
D - December 1971
1 - January 1972
2 - February 1972
3 - March 1972
4 - April 1972
5 - May 1972
6 - June 1972
7 - July 1972

Location F - Transmission Number
D - Saginaw three-speed OD
K - McKinnon Industries four-speed
C - Cleveland Powerglide
M - Muncie three-speed
R - Saginaw four-speed
T - Toledo Powerglide
K - McKinnon Industries three-speed
P - Muncie four-speed
E - McKinnon Industries Powerglide
H - Muncie Heavy-Duty

A - Cleveland Torque Drive
X - Cleveland THM 350
B - Cleveland THM 350
Y - Toledo THM 350
2 - Model Year (1972)
A-T Calendar Month:
A - January
B - February
C - March
D - April
E - May
H - June
K - July
M - August
P - September
R - October
S - November
T - December
01-31 Day of Month
Turbo Hydra-matic Code: Contains model year, model identification, and production date
72 - Year 1972
Build Date: Code of 1970 model year begins with first day of the calendar year 1969 and continues through the 1970 calendar year.

Location G - Power Steering
1 - N40 Power Steering only

Location H - Power Brakes
1 - J50 Power Brakes

Location I - Radio Option
3 - U63 AM Radio
3 - U69 AM/FM

Location J - Disc Brake Option
3 - J52 Disc Brakes

Location K - Air Conditioning Option
1 - C60 Air Conditioning

Location L - Power Window Equipment Option
Power windows were not available on 1972 Camaros

Location M - Power Seat Option
Power seats were not available on 1972 Camaros

Location N - Chevrolet Bow tie Emblem

Chapter 7

1973 Camaro

1973 Manufacturer's suggested retail price (MSRP) for base model Camaros

Model Number	Description	MSRP
1FQ87	six-cylinder Sport Coupe	$2,732.70
1FQ87	eight-cylinder Sport Coupe	2,822.70
1FS87	eight-cylinder Type LT Coupe	3,211.70

Note: Manufacturer's suggested retail price (**MSRP**) includes the factory D&H charge (including federal excise tax) and recommended dealer delivery and handling charge. This price does not include transportation charges, state and local taxes, or any accessories or optional equipment that may be ordered.

Camaro Standard Equipment

Protective inner skirts at both front and rear wheel openings; flush-and-dry rocker panels; energy-absorbing steering column; seat belts with pushbutton buckles for all passenger positions; passenger-guard door locks with deflecting lock buttons on all doors; four-way hazard flasher; dual master cylinder brake system with warning light and corrosion-resistant brake lines; latches on folding seat backs; dual-speed windshield wipers and washers; outside rearview mirror; back-up lights; side marker lights and parking lights that illuminate with headlights; padded instrument panel, sun visors, and windshield pillars; reduced-glare instrument panel top, inside windshield moldings, horn button, steering hub, and windshield wiper arms and blades; inside day-night mirror with deflecting base; lane change feature in direction signal control; safety armrests; thick-laminate windshield; soft, low-profile window control knobs and coat hooks; energy-absorbing seat backs; yielding door and window control handles; energy-absorbing instrument panel with smooth contoured knobs and levers; tire safety rim; safety door latches and hinges; uniform shift quadrant; energy-absorbing steering wheel; snag-resistant steering wheel hardware; fuel tank and filler pipe security; high-level ventilation system; built-in blended-air heater and defroster system; Magic-Mirror acrylic lacquer finish; curved solid tempered plate glass windows; two-key lock system; weather-shielded key locks; color-keyed interior trim; scuff-resistant plastic cowl side panels with molded-in ventilator grilles; quality interior features and appointments; full-view instrument panel with instruments and controls; and locking glove compartment.

Consult authorized Chevrolet Dealers or your Fleet Representative for information on accessories and extra cost of optional equipment not listed.

General Motors Corporation reserves the right to make changes at any time, without notice, in prices, colors, materials, equipment, accessories, specifications, and models, and to discontinue models.

Serial Numbers and Identification
Vehicle Identification Number (VIN)
Example: 1Q87H3N100037

1 - Make (Chevrolet)
Q - Car Line and Series (Camaro)
87 - Body Style (last two digits of model number)
H - Engine Type
        D - 250/100 L6
        F - 307/115 V-8
        H - 350/145 V-8
        K - 350/175 V-8
        L - 350/245 V-8
3 - Model Year (1973)
N - Assembly Plant

N - Norwood
L - Van Nuys

100037 - Sequential body number

Starting unit number is 100001 and up at each plant regardless of series.

Location: The vehicle identification number (VIN) is stamped on the plate attached to the top left-hand of the instrument panel.

Transmission Identification

Example: CYS3R13
CY - Type Designation
S - Source Designation
TM - three-speed, L6 engine
TM - three-speed, V-8
S - Muncie
WC - four-speed, V-8
R - Muncie
TZ - Turbo Hydra-matic, L6 engine
FB - Turbo Hydra-matic, V-8 engine
B - Cleveland
Y - Toledo
CY - Turbo Hydra-matic, V-8 engine
— - Ypsilanti

Location:
Three-speed: stamped on left side just below cover.
Four-speed: stamped on right side of case at adapter.
Powerglide, Turbo Hydra-matic (Chevrolet): stamped on right-hand side of pan.
Turbo Hydra-matic: nameplate tag on right-hand side of case.

Month:
A - January
B - February
C - March
D - April
E - May
H - June
K - July
M - August
P - September
R - October
S - November
T - December
The letter D or N following the date indicates day or night shift.

Standard wheels on 1970-73 Z28s.

Engine Identification

Example: F1013CLJ
F - Source Designation (Flint)
1013 - Production Month and Date
CLJ - Type Designation
250ci six-cylinder
CCC - Regular engine, three-speed
CCA - Regular engine, Turbo Hydra-matic (Chevrolet)

307ci eight-cylinder
CHB - Regular engine, three-speed
CHH - Regular engine, Turbo Hydra-matic (Chevrolet)

350ci eight-cylinder (RPO L65)
CKA - Optional engine, three-speed, two-barrel carburetor
CKA - Optional engine, four-speed, two-barrel carburetor
CKW - Optional engine, Turbo Hydra-matic (Chevrolet)

350ci eight-cylinder (RPO L48)
CKB - Optional engine, three-speed, four-barrel carburetor
CKB - Optional engine, four-speed, four-barrel carburetor
CKD - Optional engine, Turbo Hydra-matic (Chevrolet)

350ci eight-cylinder (RPO Z28)
CLJ - Optional engine, four-speed, four-barrel carburetor
CLK - Optional engine, Turbo Hydra-matic

Location:
Six-cylinder engine: stamped on pad on right side of cylinder block to rear of distributor
Eight-cylinder engine: stamped on pad at front right side of cylinder block

Month and Date
01 - January
02 - February
03 - March
04 - April
05 - May
06 - June
07 - July
08 - August
09 - September
10 - October
11 - November
12 - December
01-31 - Date of Month
Rear Axle Identification
Identification number is stamped on bottom left or right of axle tube adjacent to carrier housing.

1973 Camaro Standard Equipment— Exterior
Base Model
Header panel crest "C" and "Camaro"
Valance mounted parking lamp with clear lens and amber bulb
Single "Power Beam" headlamps
Bright headlamp bezel
Argent-colored one-piece radiator grille
Bright radiator grille outline molding
One-piece front bumper with dual bumper guards
License plate mounting provision in front center
Bright top and side windshield reveal molding
Two-speed windshield wipers and washers
Non-depressed park, dull chrome wiper arms and 16" blades
Front marker lamps with amber lens - no bezel
Rear marker lamps with amber lens - no bezel
Engine displacement numerals on fender (only with 350 or 396 engines)
Front fender "Camaro" nameplates
Rectangular left-hand rearview mirror
Bright chrome flush door handles
Bright wide rocker panel molding
Bright lower window sealing strip bead
Bright body lock pillar vertical seal retainer
Hubcaps
Deck lid crest "C" and "Camaro"
Bright rear window reveal moldings
Dual rear end panel mounted taillamps and back-up lamps with bright outer bezel
Rear bumper face bar to body filler

Type LT
Header panel crest "C" and "Camaro"
Valance mounted parking lamp with clear lens and amber bulb
Single "Power Beam" headlamps
Bright headlamp bezel
Argent-colored one-piece radiator grille
"Type LT" nameplate on grille (RS front end) or on left header panel extension (standard front end). (Note: Type LT emblems take precedence over any other option emblems, such as Rally Sport or Z28.)
Bright radiator grille outline molding
One-piece front bumper with dual high-rise bumper guards incorporating impact strips

License plate mounting provision in front center
Bright top and side windshield reveal molding
Two-speed windshield wipers and washers
Concealed black chrome finished wipers - articulated left arm and 18" wiper blades
Front marker lamps with amber lens - no bezel
Rear marker lamps with amber lens - no bezel
Camaro 350 identification on "Type LT"
Front fender "Camaro" nameplates
Front fender nameplate "Camaro"
Sail panel nameplate "Type LT"
Sport mirrors in body color (RPO D35) for "Type LT"
Bright chrome flush door handles
Bright lower window sealing strip bead
Bright body lock pillar vertical seal retainer
Body side lower molding on door, rear quarter, and fender with black paint below
Rally wheel and trim rings, 14"x7" (RPO ZJ7)
Deck lid crest "C" and "Camaro"
Rear end panel nameplate "Type LT" between license and right-hand inboard taillamp
Bright rear window reveal moldings
Dual rear end panel mounted taillamps and back-up lamps with bright outer bezel
Rear bumper face bar to body filler

Style Trim (RPO Z21)
Header panel crest "C" and "Camaro"
Valance mounted parking lamp with clear lens and amber bulb
Single "Power Beam" headlamps
Bright headlamp bezel
Argent-colored one-piece radiator grille
Bright radiator grille outline molding
One-piece front bumper with dual high-rise bumper guards incorporating impact strips
License plate mounting provision in front center (only for states requiring front license plates)
Bright top and side windshield reveal molding
Bright rear window reveal moldings
Two-speed windshield wipers and washers
Non-depressed park, dull chrome wiper arms and 16" blades
Bright hood and fender upper edge molding
Front marker lamps with amber lens - no bezel
Rear marker lamps with amber lens - no bezel
Engine displacement numerals on fender (only with 350 engines)
Front fender "Camaro" nameplates
Rectangular left-hand rearview mirror
Bright chrome flush door handles
Body colored tape insert on flush door handles
Bright wide rocker panel molding
Bright body lock pillar vertical molding

Bright roof drip moldings
Bright door belt reveal molding
Hubcaps
Deck lid "Camaro by Chevrolet" nameplate
Taillamps and back-up lamps with dual concentric bright bezels
Rear bumper face bar to body filler

Rally Sport (RPO Z22)
Header panel crest "C" and "Camaro"
Special parking lamp adjacent to headlamp with bright bezel and ornament
Single "Power Beam" headlamps
Bright headlamp bezel
Special two-piece, black-painted radiator grille with argent-painted leading edges
Bright radiator grille filler
Individual right-hand and left-hand front bumpers
Resilient grille frame with rubber-protected center grille section of bumper stock
License plate mounting provision below front right bumper (for states requiring front license plates)
Bright top and side windshield reveal molding
Bright rear window reveal moldings
Two-speed windshield wipers and washers
Concealed black chrome-finished wipers - articulated left arm and 18" Wiper blades
Front marker lamps with amber lens - no bezel
Rear marker lamps with amber lens - no bezel
Engine displacement numerals on fender (only with 350 engines)
Rally Sport fender nameplates (when Z28 option is combined with RS, Z28 emblems will appear. When RS or Z28 option is provided on Type LT model, Type LT emblems will appear)
Rectangular left-hand rearview mirror
Bright chrome flush door handles
Bright wide rocker panel molding
Bright lower window sealing strip bead
Bright body lock pillar vertical seal retainer
Hubcaps
Deck lid crest "C" and "Camaro"
Dual rear end panel mounted taillamps and back-up lamps with bright outer bezel
Rear bumper face bar to body filler

Z28 (RPO Z28)
Header panel crest "C" and "Camaro"
Valance mounted parking lamp with clear lens and amber bulb
Single "Power Beam" headlamps
Bright headlamp bezel
Black painted radiator grille
Bright radiator grille outline molding

Radiator grille Z28 emblem (Note: if combined with Type LT model, car will have Type LT emblems)

One-piece front bumper with dual high-rise bumper guards incorporating impact strips

License plate mounting provision in front center (only for states requiring front license plates)

Wide hood paint stripes

Bright top and side windshield reveal molding

Two-speed windshield wipers and washers

Non-depressed park, dull chrome wiper arms and 15" 6 blades

Front marker lamps with amber lens - no bezel

Rear marker lamps with amber lens - no bezel

Z28 front fender nameplates (Note: if combined with Type LT model, car will have Type LT emblems)

Rectangular left-hand rearview mirror

Bright chrome flush door handles

Bright wide rocker panel molding

Bright lower window sealing strip bead

Bright body lock pillar vertical seal retainer

White lettered wide oval 15" tires on special wheels

Deck lid crest "C" and "Camaro"

Bright rear window reveal moldings

Dual rear end panel mounted taillamps and back-up lamps with bright outer bezel

Wide paint stripes on deck lid

Rear bumper face bar to body filler

(Note: Air conditioning was available on the Z28 model for the first time ever.)

1973 Camaro Standard Equipment— Interior
Base Model

Trim color instrument panel pad

Black accented gray-painted instrument cluster

Glove compartment door lock

"Camaro" glove compartment nameplate

Black side kick-pad ventilation control knob

Black Astro-ventilation control knob

T-handle parking brake release

Instrument panel Astro-ventilation outlets

Windshield wiper and washer switch nomenclature - illuminated (slide-type, depress to wash)

Lighting control knob - black soft vinyl with symbol

Speedometer, odometer, and fuel gauge

Temperature, generator, oil pressure, and brake warning tell-tale lights

"Fasten Seat Belt" lamp in instrument panel

Hi-beam and turn signal indicators

Automatic shift quadrant cover plate

Clock hole cover

Radio hole cover

Ashtray

Cigarette lighter knob - black soft vinyl with symbol

Blended-air heater with illuminated control plate

Black steering column

Black four-spoke sport vinyl steering wheel with Chevrolet emblem at center

Steering column ignition switch with integral steering wheel and transmission lock

Black plastic hazard flasher knob

Soft black turn signal knob

One low-note horn

Premier vinyl-coated perforated headlining

Trim color windshield header, pillar, roof side rails, and rear window moldings

Black ten-inch prismatic rearview mirror with black padded edge

Black rearview mirror support, windshield mounted

Padded sunshades

Trim-colored plastic coat hooks

Center dome lamp with bright bezel

Door jamb dome lamp switches

Black front seat shoulder belt anchor covers

Front seat shoulder belt retainer - headlining color

Full foam bucket front seats with integral head restraints

Rear seat - dual cushions with single, full-width backrest full foam construction

Black front seat adjuster handle

Black front bucket seat back latch

Passenger compartment floor carpet

Luggage compartment spatter paint

Luggage compartment rubber floor mat with felt backing

Front and rear seat belts: four; Base, black with black plastic mini-buckles, locking retractors

Front shoulder belts: two; Base, black with "D" ring attachment; stowage by plastic trim color trough

Trim color seat back hinge arm cover

Injection molded lower door trim panel incorporating built-in padded armrest, front and rear map pockets, and coin receptacle

Built-in rear quarter panel armrest

Clear plastic window control handle knobs

Bright door lock buttons

Vinyl and plastic quarter trim

Soft-feel vinyl door upper trim panel

Recessed door handle

Trim colored plastic inside door handle cup

Soft black transmission shift lever knob with white shift pattern

Floor-mounted transmission shift lever

The RS front end with split bumpers and above-bumper parking lamps could be ordered on a Z28 or a plain 6-cylinder Camaro.

Long, lean European styling of the second-generation Camaro was evident in this side view.

Engine lift stop bracket setup. A service campaign was performed in the early 1970's on cars which were prone to engine mount breakage. These were normally the higher horsepower cars. A separate part number was available for small block and big block.

Type LT

Trim color instrument panel pad
Woodgrain appliqué on instrument cluster
Glove compartment door lock
"Camaro" glove compartment nameplate
Black side kick-pad ventilation control knob
Black Astro-ventilation control knob
T-handle parking brake release
Instrument panel Astro-ventilation outlets
Windshield wiper and washer switch nomenclature - illuminated (slide-type, depress to wash)
Lighting control knob - black soft vinyl with symbol
Speedometer, odometer, and fuel gauge
"Fasten Seat Belt" lamp in instrument panel
Hi-beam and turn signal indicators
Glove compartment lamp
Automatic shift quadrant cover plate
Radio hole cover
Ashtray
Cigarette lighter knob - black soft vinyl with symbol
Blended-air heater with illuminated control plate
Black steering column
Black four-spoke sport vinyl steering wheel; specific insert for Type LT
Steering column ignition switch with integral steering wheel and transmission lock
Black plastic hazard flasher knob
Soft black turn signal knob
Argent-finish accent beads on lower instrument panel
One low-note horn
Special instrumentation package (RPO U14)
Premier vinyl-coated perforated headlining
Trim color windshield header, pillar, roof side rails, and rear window moldings
Black ten-inch prismatic rearview mirror with black padded edge
Black rearview mirror support, windshield mounted
Padded sunshades
Trim-colored plastic coat hooks
Center dome lamp with bright bezel
Door jamb dome lamp switches
Black front seat shoulder belt anchor covers
Trim color front seat shoulder belt covers (requires RPO AK1 Deluxe Seat Belts and Shoulder Harnesses; not available with black interior)
Front seat shoulder belt retainer - headlining color
Full foam bucket front seats with integral head restraints
Deluxe seat trim
Rear seat - dual cushions with single, full-width backrest full foam construction
Black front seat adjuster handle
Black front bucket seat back latch
Passenger compartment floor carpet
Luggage compartment spatter paint
Luggage compartment rubber floor mat with felt backing
Front and rear seat belts: four; Base, black with black plastic mini-buckles, locking retractors
Front shoulder belts: two; Base, black with "D" ring attachment; stowage by plastic trim color trough
Trim color seat back hinge arm cover
Injection molded lower door trim panel incorporating built-in padded armrest, front and rear map pockets, and coin receptacle
Built-in rear quarter panel armrest
Clear plastic window control handle knobs
Bright door lock buttons
Vinyl and plastic quarter trim
Horizontal woodgrain insert strip on upper door trim panel between armrest and window handle with bright edges
Recessed door handle
Chrome inside door handle cup with black painted insert
Additional body insulation
Full molded hood insulation
Cowl to fender seal
Soft black transmission shift lever knob with white shift pattern
Floor-mounted transmission shift lever

Interior Decor/Quiet Sound Group (RPO Z54)

Trim color instrument panel pad
Woodgrain appliqué on instrument cluster
Glove compartment door lock
"Camaro" glove compartment nameplate
Black side kick-pad ventilation control knob

Black Astro-ventilation control knob
T-handle parking brake release
Instrument panel Astro-ventilation outlets
Windshield wiper and washer switch nomenclature - illuminated (slide-type, depress to wash)
Lighting control knob - black soft vinyl with symbol
Speedometer, odometer, and fuel gauge
Temperature, generator, oil pressure, and brake warning tell-tale lights
"Fasten Seat Belt" lamp in instrument panel
Hi-beam and turn signal indicators
Glove compartment lamp
Automatic shift quadrant cover plate
Clock hole cover
Radio hole cover
Ashtray
Cigarette lighter knob - black soft vinyl with symbol
Blended-air heater with illuminated control plate
Black steering column
Black four-spoke sport vinyl steering wheel with Chevrolet emblem at center
Steering column ignition switch with integral steering wheel and transmission lock
Black plastic hazard flasher knob
Soft black turn signal knob
One low-note horn
Additional instrument cluster lighting
Premier vinyl-coated perforated headlining
Trim color windshield header, pillar, roof side rails, and rear window moldings
Black ten-inch prismatic rearview mirror with black padded edge
Black rearview mirror support, windshield mounted
Padded sunshades
Trim-colored plastic coat hooks
Center dome lamp with bright bezel
Door jamb dome lamp switches
Black front seat shoulder belt anchor covers
Trim color front seat shoulder belt anchor covers (requires RPO AK1 Deluxe Seat Belts and Shoulder Harnesses; not available with black interior)
Front seat shoulder belt retainer - color-keyed plastic hook and clear plastic hanger
Full foam bucket front seats with integral head restraints
Rear seat - dual cushions with single, full-width backrest full foam construction
Black front seat adjuster handle
Black front bucket seat back latch
Passenger compartment floor carpet
Luggage compartment spatter paint
Luggage compartment rubber floor mat with felt backing
Front and rear seat belts: four; Base, black with black plastic mini-buckles, locking retractors
Optional front and rear seat belts: Color-coordinated belts with plastic color-keyed mini-buckles, locking retractors
Front shoulder belts: two; Base, black with "D" ring attachment; stowage by plastic trim color trough
Optional front shoulder belts: two; Color-coordinated, "D" ring attachment; stowage by plastic trim color trough
Trim color seat back hinge arm cover
Injection molded lower door trim panel incorporating built-in padded armrest, front and rear map pockets, and coin receptacle
Built-in rear quarter panel armrest
Clear plastic window control handle knobs
Bright door lock buttons
Vinyl and plastic quarter trim
Soft-feel vinyl door upper trim panel
Recessed door handle
Trim colored plastic inside door handle cup
Additional body insulation
Full molded hood insulation
Cowl to fender seal
Soft black transmission shift lever knob with white shift pattern
Floor-mounted transmission shift lever

New Features for 1973
New vinyl roof and interior color choices
Sixteen Magic-Mirror acrylic colors (fourteen new)
New standard vinyl steering wheel
Hide-A-Way antenna built into windshield glass
Full foam seat construction replacing seat springs
New stronger front bumper

Occupant Protection Features
Seat belts with pushbutton buckles for all passenger positions
Single-buckle seat and shoulder belts for driver and right front passenger with reminder light and buzzer
Two front seat head restraints
Energy-absorbing steering column
Passenger-guard door locks with forward mounted lock buttons
Safety door latches and hinges
Folding seat back latches
Energy-absorbing padded instrument panel and front seat back tops
Thick-laminate windshield
Padded sun visors
Safety armrests
Safety steering wheel

Side-guard beams
Cargo-guard luggage compartment
Contoured full-roof inner panel
Full tank impact security
Glove compartment and console door latch impact security
Yielding windshield pillar moldings
Smooth-contoured door and window regulator handles
Soft, low profile window control knobs, coat hooks, and dome light
Stamped steel door hinges
High-strength front seat anchorages and construction
High-strength rear seat retention

Accident Prevention Features
Side marker lights and reflectors (front side marker lights flash with directional signal)
Parking lights that illuminate with headlights
Four-way hazard warning flasher
Back-up lights
Lane-change feature in direction signal control
Windshield defroster, washers, and dual-speed wipers
Wide-view inside day-night mirror (vinyl-edged, shatter-resistant glass) and deflecting support
Outside rearview mirror
Dual-action safety hood latches
Dual master cylinder brake system with warning light
Headlight aiming access provision
Low-glare instrument panel top, inside windshield moldings, wiper arms and blades, and steering wheel metallic surfaces
Safety wheel rims
Uniform shift quadrant
No winged wheel nuts, discs, and caps
Self-adjusting brakes
Starter safety switch
Improved bumper system
Illumination of windshield wiper and washer, heater and defroster controls

Anti-Theft Features
Anti-theft ignition key warning buzzer
Anti-theft steering column lock
Multiple key combinations
Visible vehicle identification
Tamper-resistant odometer with telltale feature

Traditional Quality Features
Astro-Ventilation system with large rectangular vent ports on instrument panel
Side marker lights front and rear
Long hood styling

Slender full-width front bumper, silver-finish grille in large grid pattern, license plate mounting centered between front bumper guards, wide parking lights below bumper
Single-unit "Power Beam" headlights recessed in bright frames on front fenders
Wide body sill moldings
Flush mounted door handles
Recessed door handles
Swept-back roof and rear deck styling
Strato-bucket seats standard equipment
Wide (ten-inch) inside day-night rearview mirror
Outer front seat belt retractors
Acoustically engineered double-panel roof structure
Forward-mounted door lock buttons
Magic-Mirror acrylic lacquer finish
Flush-and-dry rocker panels
Curved side windows
Flush-mounted windshield and rear window bonded to body
Dual-speed electric windshield wipers
Built-in blended-air heater and defroster system
Inner fenders front and rear
108" wheelbase
Foot-operated parking brake
Deep-twist carpet floor covering
Suspended accelerator pedal
Efficient valve-in-head design
Positive shift starter
Quiet hydraulic valve lifters
Sealed side-terminal Energizer battery
Automatic choke on all engines
Advanced accessory drive system on all V-8 engines
Delcotron generator
Seven main bearing six-cylinder engine with fully counterweighted crankshaft
Transmission-controlled spark advance
Separate front frame unit
Advanced design front suspension with forward mounted steering linkage
Wide front and rear tread
Bias belted ply tires
Bias-mounted rear shock absorbers (curb side unit mounted ahead of axle, other mounted behind) for excellent suspension control
Computer-selected front and rear springs
Independent coil front suspension
Multi-leaf rear springs
Disc brakes standard on front wheels (power operation optional)
Finned rear brake drums
Self-adjusting brakes
Precise Ball-Race steering

1973 Camaro Options and Accessories

When Factory Installed
V-8 Models (115hp Turbo-Fire 307 V-8)

1FQ87 Sport Coupe	$2,822.70
1FS87 Type LT Coupe	3,211.70

Six-cylinder Models (100hp Turbo-Thrift 250 Six)

1FQ87 Sport Coupe	2,732.70

Z54

Interior Decor/Quiet Sound: includes glove compartment light and additional instrument cluster lighting; woodgrain accents on instrument cluster; and special engine compartment, hood, and interior insulation (standard with Type LT) $35.00

Z22

Rally Sport: includes special black-finished grille with special rubber-tipped vertical center bar and resilient body color grille frame; independent left-hand and right-hand front bumpers replacing full-width bumper; parking lights with bright accents mounted on grille panel; Hide-A-Way windshield wipers (Rally Sport emblems deleted with Z28 Special Performance Package) $118.00
with Type LT $97.00

Z21

Style Trim: includes bright roof drip, lock pillar, upper fender, hood panel and belt moldings, plus color door handle inserts, bright-accented parking lights, taillights, and back-up lights $56.00

Z28

Special Performance Package: includes 245hp Turbo-Fire special 350ci V-8 with finned aluminum rocker covers and bright accents; increased cooling; power brakes; dual exhausts; black-finished grille; sport suspension; heavy-duty starter and clutch; 15"x7" wheels with bright lug nuts, special center caps and trim rings; F60-15B bias belted ply white letter tires; posi-traction rear axle (V-8 model with four-speed or Turbo Hydra-matic transmission only; not available with wheel covers or rally wheels; air conditioning not available with four-speed) $598.05
with Type LT $502.05

Nice view of the inner-workings of a 12-bolt Camaro rear end. The 1967-69 Camaro rear length was shorter than its 1970-73 counterpart.

Power Teams

Engines: See Power Team chart for complete engine specifications, model and transmission availability.

L48	175hp Turbo-Fire 350ci V-8 (available only with power brakes)	102.00
	with Type LT	76.00
L65	145hp Turbo-Fire 350ci V-8 (standard with Type LT)	26.00

Transmissions: See Power Team chart for availability

M40	Turbo Hydra-matic automatic	210.00
	with Z28 Special Performance Package	297.00
M20	Four-speed wide range transmission (not available with base six or base V-8 engine)	200.00
M21	Four-speed close ratio transmission (available only with Z28 Special Performance Package; not available with air conditioning)	200.00
G80	Posi-traction Rear Axle (included with Z28 Special Performance Package)	45.00

Axle Ratios:

YD1	Special axle ratio for trailering (requires base V-8 or RPO L65 engines and automatic transmission)	12.00

Power Assists

J50	Power Steering (included with Z28 Special Performance Package)	46.00
N40	Power Brakes, variable ratio (standard with Type LT)	113.00

Other Options

C50   Air Conditioning, Four Season: V-8 models only, includes 61-amp generator and heavy-duty radiator. Requires power brakes, not available with close ratio four-speed   97.00

T60   Heavy-Duty Battery, 15-plate, 80 amp-hr   15.00

AK1   Custom Deluxe Seat and Shoulder Belts, includes color-keyed belts and plastic buckles (available only with chamois, green, neutral, or saddle interiors)   14.50

YA7   California Emission Equipment   15.00

U35   Electric Clock (included with special instrumentation or Type LT)   16.00

V01   Heavy-Duty Radiator (included with air conditioning)   14.00

with Z28 Special Performance Package   7.50

VQ1   Coolant Recovery System

D55   Console: includes floor-mounted shift lever (when automatic transmission is ordered), rear seat courtesy and compartment lights   57.00

C50   Rear Window Defroster   31.00

B37   Color Keyed Front and Rear Floor Mats   12.00

A01   Soft-Ray Tinted Glass, all windows   39.00

B93   Door Edge Guards   6.00

U14   Special Instrumentation: includes tachometer, ammeter, and temperature gauges plus electric clock mounted in instrument cluster, and additional instrument cluster lighting (V-8 models only, included with Type LT)   82.00

ZJ9   Auxiliary Lighting: includes ashtray, courtesy, luggage compartment, and glove compartment lights   17.50

Type LT or Interior Decor Package   15.00

D34   Vanity Visor Mirror   3.00

D35   Sport Mirrors: includes left-hand remote control and right-hand manual (included with Type LT or Z28 Special Performance Package)   26.00

B84   Body Side Molding   33.00

U63   AM Radio   65.00

U69   AM/FM Radio   135.00

U80   Rear Seat Speaker   15.00

C08   Vinyl Roof Cover, includes bright roof drip molding
AA - White
BB - Black
DD - Blue
FF - Chamois
GG - Green
HH - Red
TT - Neutral   87.00

AN6   Adjustable Seat Back, two positions (driver's side only)   18.00

N65   Space Saver Spare Tire   14.16

Credit with E78-14 tires and Turbine wheels   0.84

Credit with F70-14 tires and Turbine wheels   0.60

Credit with Z28 Special Performance Package   0.60

Add with F70-14 tires without Turbine wheels   14.40

D80   Spoilers, Front and Rear: includes front valance spoiler, rear deck, and side panel spoiler; front spoiler shipped loose for dealer installation   77.00

D88   Sport Stripes: includes hood and rear deck striping (available only with Z28 Special Performance Package; not available with Type LT)   77.00

N33   Comfortilt Steering Wheel   44.00

F41   Sport Suspension: includes special front stabilizer, rear stabilizer, and special front and rear shock absorbers (V-8 models with F70-14B tires only; included with Z28 Special Performance Package)   30.00

ZJ4   Trailer Towing Package: includes heavy-duty radiator, extra cooling fan, 3.42:1 axle (requires base V-8 or RPO L65 engine and automatic transmission)   41.00

C24   Hide-A-Way Windshield Wipers: includes articulated left-hand blade (included with Rally Sport or Type LT)   21.00

A31   Power Windows   75.00

N95   Wheel Covers: Wire, not available with Type LT   82.00

P01   Wheel Covers: Bright Metal, not available with Type LT   26.00

PE1   Turbine Wheels, 14"x7" (not available with Z28 Special Performance Package)   110.50

with Type LT   75.00

ZJ7   Rally Wheels: includes special 14"x7" wheels, hub-caps, and trim rings (standard with Type LT; not available on V-8 Sport Coupe with E78x14B tires)   44.00

QEH   Tires, E78-14B bias belted white stripe   28.00

with Space Saver spare tire   22.40

QFC   Tires, F70-14B bias belted white stripe (V-8 models only)   70.00

with Sport Coupe and Space Saver spare tire   56.00

with Type LT without Space Saver spare tire   65.00

with Type LT and Space Saver spare tire   51.00

QFD   Tires, F70-14B bias belted white letter, includes 14"x7" wheels (V-8 models only)   83.00

with Sport Coupe and Space Saver spare tire   66.40

with Type LT without Space Saver spare tire   78.00

with Type LT and Space Saver spare tire   61.40

Dealer-Installed Custom Features and Accessories

Description	Part No.
Radio Antenna, front mounted	994316
Citizens Band Radio	994461
Battery Blanket	992191
Power Brakes	994434
Locking Gas Cap	994171
GM Infant Safety Carrier	994259
Auto Compass	993915
Litter Container and Tissue Dispenser, Saddle-type	
Black	994476
Dark Blue	994477
Dark Green	994478
Beige	994479
Wheel Covers, 14"	994458
Simulated Wire Wheel Covers, 14"	994206
Simulated Mag Wheel Covers, 14"	993722
Rear Window Defogger	994324
Highway Emergency Kit	993537
Fire Extinguisher	994334
Fire Extinguisher Recharge Kit	985593
Rear Bumper Guards	993972
Door Edge Guards, stainless	993964
Door Edge Guards, vinyl, universal	994330
Fender Guards, front or rear, pair	993985
Fender Flares, front pair	994483
Fender Flares, rear pair	994484
Trailer Wiring Harness	994532
Engine Block Heater, except 396 and 454	994161
Engine Block Heater, with 396 and 454	994162
Frame Mounted Trailer Hitch	994474
Lights	
Glove Compartment	993982
Luggage Compartment	993997
Under-hood	994317
Hood Pin Locks with key	994203
Contour Floor Mats	
Black, front	989096
Black, rear	989103
Dark Blue, front	989120
Dark Blue, rear	989125
Dark Saddle, front	989121
Dark Saddle, rear	989126
Dark Green, front	989122
Dark Green, rear	989127
Midnight Blue, front	994416
Midnight Blue, rear	981879
Dark Oxblood, front	989123
Dark Oxblood, rear	989128
Midnight Neutral, front	989124
Midnight Neutral, rear	989130
Medium Dark Chamois, front	994422
Medium Dark Chamois, rear	994432
Right-hand Rearview Mirror	994039
Trailering Mirrors, pair	NPN
Vanity Visor Mirror	994521
Vinyl Side Molding Units, two-17 ft. rolls	
Black	994408
Medium Blue	994404
Light Green	994405
Red	994406
Chamois	994407
AM/FM Stereo Radio/Tape Combination	994322
AM Radio/Tape Player Combination	994321
AM/FM Pushbutton Radio	994363
AM/FM Stereo Radio	994364
AM Pushbutton Radio	994362
Rear Speakers, pair	994121
Hand Portable Spotlight	987112
Interior Warmer	994264

1973 Camaro Trim Plate

```
ST 73 (A) 1FQ87 (B)      N(C)      171489 BDY (D)
TR 775 (E)    A51(F)        68 (G)-68 (H) PNT
04E (I)   Z28 (J)   YF8 (K)
510393 (L)
```

Location A - Model Year
73 - 1973

Location B - Body Style
1FQ87 - Sport Coupe
1FS87 - Type LT Coupe

Location C - Assembly Plant
NOR - Norwood, Ohio
BL - Van Nuys, California

Location D - Sequential Body Number
The number assigned to that particular body at the assembly plant

Location E - Interior Trim Code
773 - Black vinyl, Type LT
774 - Blue/Black pattern cloth, Sport Coupe

Rear seat speaker was available on AM-radio cars.

775 - Black vinyl, Sport Coupe
776 - Black/White pattern cloth, Sport Coupe
777 - Dark Green vinyl, Sport Coupe
778 - Dark Saddle vinyl, Sport Coupe
779 - Light Neutral vinyl, Sport Coupe
780 - Medium Chamois vinyl, Sport Coupe
781 - Dark Green/Black pattern cloth, Type LT
785 - Black/White pattern cloth, Type LT
786 - Blue/Black pattern cloth, Type LT

Location F - Seat Type
A51 - Front Strato-Bucket Seats

Location G - Lower Body Paint Code
The first number indicates lower body color
11 - Antique White
24 - Light Blue Metallic
26 - Dark Blue Metallic
29 - Midnight Blue Metallic
42 - Dark Green Metallic
44 - Light Green Metallic
46 - Green Gold Metallic
48 - Midnight Green
51 - Light Yellow
56 - Chamois
60 - Light Copper Metallic
64 - Silver Metallic
68 - Dark Brown Metallic
74 - Dark Red Metallic
75 - Medium Red
97 - Medium Orange Metallic

Location H - Upper Body Paint Code/Vinyl Top Code
A number here would designate no vinyl top. The number should match the lower body color number.
AA - White

BB - Black
DD - Medium Blue
FF - Chamois
GG - Medium Green
HH - Maroon
TT - Light Neutral

Location I - Build Date Code
01 - January
02 - February
03 - March
04 - April
05 - May
06 - June
07 - July
08 - August
09 - September
10 - October
11 - November
12 - December
A - 1st week of month
B - 2nd week of month
C - 3rd week of month
D - 4th week of month
E - 5th week of month

Location J - Option Code
Norwood cars only - No designation here would tell you only that the car is not a Norwood Z28.
Z28 - RPO Z28

Location K - Z28 Stripe Color
Norwood cars only
ZR8 - White hood and deck striping
YF8 - Black hood and deck striping

Location L - Undefined at this time on both Norwood and Van Nuys cars.

1973 Camaro Protect-O-Plate
There was no Protect-O-Plate furnished with 1973 and up Camaros.

The front spoiler on a 70-73 standard Z28 was different than a Rally Sport car.

Paint and Trim Combinations

1967 Camaro Exterior Color and Interior Trim Chart

INTERIOR TRIM COLORS AND RPO NUMBERS

			Gold	Blue	Black	Turq.	Brt. Red	Parch-ment/ Blue	Black	Yellow
						Models 12437-12467				
			709	717	760	—	741	—	—	—
						Deluxe Bucket Seat Option				
			711	—	765	779	742	732	797	707
						Sport Coupe Standard Interior Bench Seat Option				
			796	739	756	—	—	—	—	—
	EXTERIOR					**Sport Coupe Deluxe Interior Bench Seat Option**				
RPO	COLOR		712	—	767	—	716	—	—	—
AA	Tuxedo Black	(W)	X	X	X	X	X	X	X	X
CC	Ermine White	(B)	X	X	X	X	X	X	X	X
DD	Nantucket Blue	(W)	—	X	X	—	—	X	X	—
EE	Deepwater Blue	(W)	—	X	X	—	—	X	X	—
FF	Marina Blue	(W)*	—	X	X	—	—	X	X	—
GG	Granada Gold	(B)	X	—	X	—	—	—	X	X
HH	Mountain Green	(B)	—	—	X	—	—	—	X	—
KK	Emerald Turquoise	(B)	—	—	X	X	—	—	X	—
LL	Tahoe Turquoise	(W)	—	—	X	X	—	—	X	—
MM	Royal Plum	(W)	—	—	X	—	—	—	X	—
NN	Madeira Maroon	(W)	X	—	X	—	X	—	X	—
RR	Bolero Red	(W)*	—	—	X	—	X	—	X	—
SS	Sierra Fawn	(B)	X	—	X	—	—	—	X	X
TT	Capri Cream	(B)	X	—	X	—	—	—	X	X
YY	Butternut Yellow	(B)	—	—	X	X	X	—	X	X

Convertible top: White (regular production), black, or medium blue (RPO CO5) with any exterior color.

Vinyl top option (RPO CO8): Black or light fawn with any exterior color.

Body side and front header panel paint stripe color for SS350 option, Rally Sport Option, and the optional Style trim Group: (W) white, (B) black.

*Bolero Red and Marina Blue Camaros with black vinyl or convertible tops will have black paint stripes.

1968 Camaro Exterior Color and Interior Trim Chart

SERIES	Cpe	Conv	TRIM	Black	Blue	Gold	Red	Turquoise	Parch/Blk	Blk/White
Standard	x	x	Vinyl Bucket	712	717	722	724	—	—	—
Custom	x		Vinyl Bench Opt.	713	718	723	—	—	—	—
Interior	x	x	Vinyl Bucket	714	719	721	725	726	730	—
RPO Z87	x		Vinyl Bench Opt.	715	720	—	—	727	—	—
			Cloth Bkt Opt - Houndstooth	—	—	—	—	—	—	749t

RPO	EXTERIOR COLOR		Black	Blue	Gold	Red	Turquoise	Parch/Blk	Blk/White
AA	Tuxedo Black	W*(a)	X	X	X	X	X	X	X
CC	Ermine White	B	X	X	X	X	X	X	X
DD	Grotto Blue	W	X	X	—	—	—	X	X
EE	Fathom Blue	W*	X	X	—	—	—	X	X
FF	Island Teal	W	X	—	—	—	—	X	X
GG	Ash Gold	B	X	—	X	—	—	X	X
HH	Grecian Green	B*	X	—	—	—	—	X	X
JJ	Rallye Green	W*	X	—	—	—	—	X	X
KK	Tripoli Turquoise	B	X	—	—	—	X	X	X
LL	Teal Blue	W	X	X	—	—	—	X	X
NN	Cordovan Maroon	W	X	—	—	X	—	X	X
OO	Corvette Bronze	B*	X	—	—	—	—	X	X
PP	Seafrost Green	B	X	—	X	—	—	X	X
RR	Matador Red	W(b)	X	—	—	X	—	X	X
TT	Palomino Ivory	B*	X	—	X	—	—	X	X
UU	LeMans Blue	W*	X	X	—	—	—	X	X
VV	Sequoia Green	W	X	—	X	—	—	X	X
YY	Butternut Yellow	B	X	—	X	—	—	X	X
ZZ	British Green	W*	X	—	X	—	—	X	X

Convertible top: White (regular production), black, or blue (RPO CO5) with any exterior color.

Vinyl top (CO8): Black or white with any exterior color.

(a) Body paint color stripes—W=white, B=black

(b) Paint stripe color will be black if ordered with black vinyl or convertible top.

*A revision in January 1968 deleted AA Tuxedo Black, EE Fathom Blue, HH Grecian Green, and TT Palomino Ivory. At that time the following colors were added: JJ Rallye Green, OO Corvette Bronze, UU LeMans Blue, and ZZ British Green.

Note: Black/White interior refers to optional Houndstooth upholstery. The January 1968 revision introduced the white vinyl/black and white Houndstooth interior. Until that point, only black vinyl/black and white Houndstooth was available. When white vinyl/black and white Houndstooth was ordered, the balance of the interior components remained black.

1969 Camaro Exterior Color and Interior Trim Chart

SERIES	TRIM	BLack	Dark Blue	Med. Green	Dark Green	Med Red	Parch-ment
Standard	Vinyl (buckets)	711	715	721	723	718	727
RPO Z87	Vinyl (buckets)	712	716	722	725	719	
Custom Interior	Cloth (buckets)*	713					729

Los Angeles	Nor-wood	RPO	EXTERIOR COLOR	Black	Dark Blue	Med Green	Dark Green	Med Red	Parch-ment
S.O.	X	10	Tuxedo Black	X	X	X	X	X	X
S.O.	S.O.	40	Butternut Yellow	X	—	—	X	—	X
X	X	50	Dover White	X	X	X	X	X	X
S.O.	X	51	Dusk Blue	X	X	—	—	—	X
X	X	52	Garnet Red	X	—	—	—	X	X
X	X	53	Glacier Blue	X	X	—	—	—	X
X	X	55	Azure Turquoise	X	—	—	—	—	X
X	X	57	Fathom Green	X	—	X	X	—	X
X	X	59	Frost Lime	X	—	X	X	—	X
S.O.	X	61	Burnished Brown	X	—	—	—	—	X
X	S.O.	63	Champagne	X	—	—	X	—	X
X	X	65	Olympic Gold	X	—	—	X	—	X
S.O.	X	67	Burgundy Maroon	X	—	—	—	X	X
X	X	69	Cortez Silver	X	X	—	X	X	X
X	X	71	LeMans Blue	X	—	—	—	X	X
X	X	72	Hugger Orange	X	—	—	—	—	X
X	X	76	Daytona Yellow	X	—	—	—	—	X
X	X	79	Rallye Green	X	—	—	—	—	X
S.O.	X	51-53	Dusk Blue/Glacier Blue	X	X	—	—	—	X
X	X	53-50	Glacier Blue/Dover Wh	X	X	—	—	—	X
S.O.	X	53-51	Glacier Blue/Dusk Blue	X	X	—	—	—	X
X	X	55-50	Azure Turq./Dover White	X	—	—	—	—	X
S.O.	S.O.	61-63	Burn Brown/Champagne	X	—	—	—	—	X
X	X	65-60	Olympic Gold/Dover Wh	X	—	—	X	—	X

* denotes Houndstooth pattern
S.O. denotes special order
Two-tone paint not available on convertible models

Midnight Green	SS	Tuxedo Black
		Dover White
		Frost Green
		Fathom Green

1969 Camaro Exterior Color and Interior Trim Chart (continued)
Vinyl Roof Color Choices (RPO C08)

Vinyl Roof Availability Color	Code	Exterior Color
Black	BB	All
Parchment	EE	All
Dark Brown	FF	Olympic Gold
		Butternut Yellow
		Champagne
		Burnished Brown
Dark Blue	CC	Dover White
		Glacier Blue
		Dusk Blue
		Cortez Silver

Convertible Top Color Choices
Choice of white or black convertible top available with all exterior colors

Seat and Shoulder Belt Colors

Interior Trim Color	Standard Style Belts	Custom Deluxe Belts*
Black	Black	Black
Blue	Dark Blue	Dark Blue
Medium Green	Dark Green	Dark Green
Ivory/Black	Black	Black
Red	Black	Red
Midnight Green	Dark Green	Midnight Green

Black/Houndstooth   Black   Black
Ivory/Houndstooth   Black   Black

*Available at extra cost
Note: Standard seat and shoulder belt buckles color-keyed. Custom Deluxe buckles brush-finished.

Camaro Color Accents
Sport Striping (RPO D90)*, Front Accent Striping

(RPO DX1)**, Fender Striping (RPO D96)***

*Included on Camaro SS
** Not available on Camaro SS
*** Included with Rally Sport (RPO Z22) except when ordered with SS equipment
(a) Red with black interior
(b) Red with red interior

Sport Coupe with Vinyl Roof Cover   Convertible

Exterior Color	Sport Coupe with out Vinyl Roof	Black	Parchment	Dark Brown	Dark Blue	Midnight Green	Black Top	White Top—
Tuxedo Black	White (a)	White	White	—	—	White	White	White
Dover White	Black (b)	Black	Black	—	Black	Black	Black	Black
Glacier Blue	Black	Black	White	—	Black	—	Black	White
Dusk Blue	White	White	White	—	White	—	White	White
LeMans Blue	Black	Black	White	—	—	—	Black	White
Olympic Gold	Black	Black	White	Black	—	—	Black	White
Burnish. Brown	White	White	White	White	—	—	White	White
Azure Turquoise	Black	Black	White	—	—	—	Black	White
Frost Green	Black	Black	White	—	—	Black	Black	White
Burgundy	Red	Red	White	—	—	—	Red	White
Cortez Silver	Black (b)	Black	White	—	Black	—	Black	White
Garnet Red	Black	Black	White	—	—	—	Black	White
Champagne	Black	Black	White	Black	—	—	Black	White
Fathom Green	White	White	White	—	—	White	White	White
Butternut Yellow	Black	Black	Black	Black	—	—	Black	Black
Hugger Orange	White	Black	White	—	—	—	Black	White
Daytona Yellow	Black	Black	Black	—	—	—	Black	Black
Rallye Green	White	Black	White	—	—	—	Black	White

1970 Camaro Exterior Color and Interior Trim Chart

SERIES	TRIM	Black	Sandalwood	Saddle	Bright Blue	Dark Green
Standard	Vinyl	711	710	726	715	723
RPO Z87	Knit Vinyl	712	730	727	716	724
Custom Interior	Pattern Cloth*	713/725	—	—	714	720

RPO	EXTERIOR COLOR	Black	Sandalwood	Saddle	Bright Blue	Dark Green
10	Classic White	X	X	X	X	X
14	Cortez Silver	X	X	X	X	X
17	Shadow Gray	X	X	X	—	X
25	Astro Blue X	X	—	—	—	—
26	Mulsanne Blue	X	X	X	X	—
43	Citrus Green	X	X	—	—	X
45	Green Mist X	X	X	—	X	—
48	Forest Green	X	X	X	—	X
51	Daytona Yellow	X	—	—	—	X
53	Camaro Gold	X	X	—	—	—
58	Autumn Gold	X	X	X	—	X
63	Desert Sand	X	X	X	—	X
65	Hugger Orange	X	X	—	—	—
67	Classic Copper	X	X	X	—	—
75	Cranberry X	X	X	—	—	—

* 713 - Black/White, 725 - Black/Black, 714 - Bright Blue/Black, 720 - Dark Green/Black

1971 Camaro Exterior Color and Interior Trim Chart
Interior Colors and RPO Numbers

SERIES	TRIM	Black	Dark Blue	Dark Jade	Dark Saddle	Sandalwood	White/Black
Standard	Vinyl	775	776	778	779	777	—
RPO Z87	Pattern	785*	786*	787*	792*	—	789
Custom Interior	Cloth						

RPO	EXTERIOR COLOR						
11	Antique White	X	X	X	X	X	
13	Nevada Silver	X	X	—	—	X	
19	Tuxedo Black	X	X	X	X	X	
24	Ascot Blue	X	X	—	—	—	
26	Mulsanne Blue	X	X	—	—	—	
42	Cottonwood Green	X	—	X	—	X	
43	Lime Green	X	—	X	X	X	
49	Antique Green	X	—	X	X	X	
52	Sunflower Yellow	X	—	X	X	X	
53	Placer Gold	X	—	—	X	X	
61	Sandalwood	X	—	X	X	X	
62	Burnt Orange	X	—	—	—	X	
67	Classic Copper	X	—	—	—	X	
75	Cranberry Red	X	—	—	—	X	
78	Rosewood Metallic	X	—	—	—	X	

* 789 - Black/White, 785 - Black/Black, 786 - Dark Blue/Black, 787 - Dark Jade/Black, 792 - Dark Saddle/Black

1972 Camaro Exterior Color and Interior Trim Chart
Interior Colors and RPO Numbers

SERIES	TRIM	Black	Dark Blue	Dark Green	Medium Tan	Light Convertible	White
Standard	Vinyl	775	776	777	778	779	780
RPO Z87	Pattern	785	786	787		788	
Deluxe Interior	Cloth*						

RPO	EXT. COLOR						
11	Antique White	X	X	X	X	X	X
14	Pewter Silver	X	—	X	X	—	X
24	Ascot Blue	X	X	—	—	—	X
26	Mulsanne Blue	X	X	—	—	—	X
36	Spring Green	X	—	—	—	—	X
43	Gulf Green	X	—	X	—	X	X
48	Sequoia Green	X	—	X	X	X	X
50	Convertible Tan	X	—	X	X	X	X
53	Placer Gold	X	—	—	—	X	X
56	Cream Yellow	X	—	—	X	X	X
57	Golden Brown	X	—	—	X	X	X
63	Mohave Gold	X	—	—	X	X	X
65	Orange Flame	X	—	—	—	—	X
68	Midnight Bronze	X	—	—	X	X	X
75	Cranberry Red	X	—	—	—	—	X

Wheels were body color with hub caps, black with wheel covers, argent with RPO rally wheels, and dark gray with Z28.

1972 Camaro Exterior Color and Interior Trim Chart (continued)
Vinyl Roof and Body Stripe Colors

VINYL ROOF COLOR CHOICES

COLOR CODE	EXTERIOR COLOR	BLACK VINYL ROOF	WHITE VINYL ROOF	MEDIUM GREEN VINYL ROOF	LIGHT CONVERTIBLE VINYL ROOF	MEDIUM TAN VINYL ROOF
11	Antique White	X	X	X	X	X
14	Pewter Silver	X	X	X	—	—
24	Ascot Blue	X	X	—	—	—
26	Mulsanne Blue	X	X	—	—	—
36	Spring Green	X	X	—	—	—
43	Gulf Green	X	X	X	—	—
48	Sequoia Green	X	X	X	X	—
50	Convertible Tan	X	X	—	X	—
53	Placer Gold	X	X	—	X	—
56	Cream Yellow	X	X	—	X	—
57	Golden Brown	X	X	—	X	—
63	Mohave Gold	X	X	—	X	X
65	Orange Flame	X	X	—	X	—
68	Midnight Bronze	X	X	—	X	X
75	Cranberry Red	X	X	—	—	—

BODY STRIPE CHOICES

COLOR CODE	EXTERIOR COLOR	STRIPE COLOR
11	Antique White	Black
14	Pewter Silver	Black/White
24	Ascot Blue	Black/White
26	Mulsanne Blue	Black/White
36	Spring Green	Black/White
43	Gulf Green	Black/White
48	Sequoia Green	Black/White
50	Convertible Tan	Black/White
53	Placer Gold	Black/White
56	Cream Yellow	Black/White
57	Golden Brown	Black/White
63	Mohave Gold	Black/White
65	Orange Flame	Black/White
68	Midnight Bronze	White
75	Cranberry Red	Black/White

Vinyl top codes: AA - White, BB - Black, DD - Medium Blue, FF - Chamois, GG - Medium Green, HH - Maroon, TT - Light Neutral
Chart uses only one letter for color designation

1973 Camaro Exterior Color and Interior Trim Chart
Interior Colors and RPO Numbers

SERIES	TRIM	Medium Chamois	Blue/Black- Black Carpet	Blue/Black- Blue Carpet	Vinyl Top Choices	Stripe Colors
Standard	Vinyl	780	—	—	—	—
1FQ87	Cloth	—	774	774	—	—
Type LT	Vinyl	—	—	—	—	—
1FS87	Cloth	—	786	786	—	—

RPO	EXT. COLOR					
11	Antique White	X	X	X	B,A,G,D,F,H	Black
24	Light Blue Metallic	—	X	X	B,A,D	Black/White
26	Dark Blue Metallic	—	X	X	B,AD	Black/White
29	Midnight Blue Met.	—	X	X	B,A,D	Black/White
42	Dark Green Met.	—	—	—	B,A	Black/White
44	Light Green Met.	—	—	—	B,A,G	Black/White
46	Green Gold Met.	—	—	—	B,A,T	Black/White
48	Midnight Green	X	—	—	B,A,G,T	Black/White
51	Light Yellow	—	—	—	B,A	Black/White
56	Chamois	X	—	—	B,A,F	Black/White
60	Light Copper Met.	—	—	—	B,A,T	Black/White
64	Silver Metallic	X	X	X	B,A,H	Black/White
68	Dark Brown Met.	—	—	—	B,A,T	White
74	Dark Red Metallic	—	X	X	B,A,T,H	Black/White
75	Medium Red	—	X	X	B,A,T	Black/White
97	Med Orange Met.	—	—	—	B,A,T	Black/White

1973 Camaro Exterior Color and Interior Trim Chart (continued)
Vinyl Roof and Body Stripe Colors

VINYL ROOF COLOR CHOICES

COLOR CODE	EXTERIOR COLOR	BLACK VINYL ROOF	WHITE VINYL ROOF	MEDIUM GREEN VINYL ROOF	LIGHT CONVERTIBLE VINYL ROOF	MEDIUM TAN VINYL ROOF
11	Antique White	X	X	X	X	X
14	Pewter Silver	X	X	X	—	—
24	Ascot Blue	X	X	—	—	—
26	Mulsanne Blue	X	X	—	—	—
36	Spring Green	X	X	—	—	—
43	Gulf Green	X	X	X	—	—
48	Sequoia Green	X	X	X	X	—
50	Convertible Tan	X	X	—	X	—
53	Placer Gold	X	X	—	X	—
56	Cream Yellow	X	X	—	X	—
57	Golden Brown	X	X	—	X	—
63	Mohave Gold	X	X	—	X	X
65	Orange Flame	X	X	—	X	—
68	Midnight Bronze	X	X	—	X	X
75	Cranberry Red	X	X	—	—	—

BODY STRIPE CHOICES

COLOR CODE	EXTERIOR COLOR	STRIPE COLOR
11	Antique White	Black
14	Pewter Silver	Black/White
24	Ascot Blue	Black/White
26	Mulsanne Blue	Black/White
36	Spring Green	Black/White
43	Gulf Green	Black/White
48	Sequoia Green	Black/White
50	Convertible Tan	Black/White
53	Placer Gold	Black/White
56	Cream Yellow	Black/White
57	Golden Brown	Black/White
63	Mohave Gold	Black/White
65	Orange Flame	Black/White
68	Midnight Bronze	White
75	Cranberry Red	Black/White

Exterior Paint Processes

Rustproofing

Assembled auto bodies are chemically sprayed to clean and etch the metal surfaces for corrosion resistance and paint adhesion. Unassembled sheet metal parts follow the same procedure.

Body and Sheet Metal Primers

Four specially formulated corrosion-resistant primers are hand-sprayed on the body in areas where rust may develop. Lower areas, which are considered especially vulnerable, are coated with another rust-inhibiting compound.

Primer Coat

Applied to all outer and inner surfaces of front fenders and hood. The parts are mechanically dipped or flow-coated to insure coating in all seams and other secluded areas. Parts are baked at 390 degrees F for thirty minutes. A coat of sealer is then hand-sprayed on all surfaces requiring another coat of lacquer.

Flash Primer and Primer Surfacer Coats

An air-dry flash primer coat is hand sprayed on surfaces below the body beltline. A gray primer-surfacer coat is then hand sprayed on all outside surfaces of the body and oven baked for forty-five minutes at 285 degrees F.

Initial Sanding

Power wet sanding is done on all body surfaces requiring lacquering. This procedure is followed by hand sanding, which insures a smooth surface for the lacquer finish. To remove the water, the body is wiped and run through an infra-red oven.

Lacquering

Three coats of acrylic lacquer are spread on the exterior surfaces of the body and sheet metal parts to build up a finish of the required thickness for each color.

Initial Baking

The body and sheet metal parts are baked for approximately ten minutes at 200 degrees F to harden the paint for final sanding.

Final Sanding

Power and hand sanding is performed with fine grit sandpaper and mineral spirits as a wetting agent to remove body surface defects. Sanded areas are wiped to insure a clean surface before final baking.

Final Baking

To assure a durable, hard high-luster finish, the lacquer is baked for thirty minutes at 275 degrees F. Reheating the lacquer after final sanding permits paint film to soften, allowing surface blemishes and sanding scratches to disappear during the thermo-reflow process.

Undercoating

To block out road noise, an asbestos fiber sound deadener with asphalt base is sprayed inside the wheel housings and on the bottom of the underbody at designated areas.

Paint Repair and Protection

Mars, nicks, or scratches that occur during final assembly are corrected at the factory before shipment. When required, light "slush" polishing brings painted surfaces to a high luster finish. Wax is applied to all horizontal surfaces of each vehicle and polished out for protection during shipment. The wax contains no silicones, thus eliminating any paint contamination problem.

Appendix B

Engine and Transmission Teams

1967 Power Teams

ENGINE	TRANSMISSION	MODEL APPLICATION	REAR AXLE RATIO							
			Without air conditioning				With air conditioning			
			Std	Econ	Perf	Spec	Std	Econ	Perf	Spec
Standard 6 **145-hp Turbo-** **Thrift 230** **230 cu in Six**	Std 3-spd	All models	3.08	2.73	3.55		3.08		3.55	
	Wide Range 4-spd	All models	3.08	2.73	3.55		3.08		3.55	
	Powerglide	All models	2.73 *		3.55		3.08		3.55	
RPO L22 **155-hp Turbo-** **Thrift 250** **6-cylinder**	Std 3-spd	All models	3.08	2.73	3.55		3.08		3.55	
	Wide Range 4-spd	All models	3.08	2.73	3.55		3.08		3.55	
	Powerglide	All models	2.73 *		3.55		3.08		3.55	
Standard V8 **210 hp Turbo-** **Fire 327** **8-cylinder**	Std 3-spd	All models	3.08	2.73	3.55		3.08		3.55	
	Wide-Range 4-spd	All models	3.08	2.73	3.55		3.08		3.55	
	Powerglide	All models	2.73 *		3.55		3.08		3.55	
RPO L30 **275-hp Turbo-** **Fire 327** **8-cylinder**	Std 3-spd	All models	3.08	2.73	3.55		3.08		3:55	
	Wide Range 4-spd	All models	3.31	2.73	3.55		3.31		3.55	
	Powerglide	All models	2.73 *		3.55		3.08		3.55	
RPO L48 **Camaro SS** **option** **295-hp Turbo-** **Fire 350** **8-cylinder**	Std 3-spd	All models	3.31	3.07	3.55		3.31	3.07	3.55	
	Wide Range 4-spd	All models	3.31	3.07	3.55	3.73 4.10 4.56 4.88	3.31	3.07	3.55	
	Powerglide & Special 3-spd	All models	3.31	3.07	3.55	3.73	3.31	3.07	3.55	3.73
RPO L35 **Camaro SS** **Option** **325-hp Turbo-** **Jet 396** **8-cylinder**	Special 3-spd and Wide-range 4-spd	All models	3.07	2.73	3.31		Air Conditioning Not Available			
	Turbo Hydramatic	All models	3.73 **		2.07					

RPO L78 Camaro SS Option 375-hp Turbo-Jet 396 8-cylinder	Special 3-spd fully syncho	All models	3.07	2.73 3.31 3.55 3.73	Air Conditioning Not Available
	4-spd close ratio	All models	3.07	2.73 3.31 3.55 4.11 4.56 4.88	
RPO Z28 Camaro Z28 Option 290-hp 302 cubic inch 8-cylinder	4 spd close ratio	8-cylinder Coupe only	3.73	3.07 3.31 3.55 4.10 4.56 4.88	Air Conditioning Not Available

* 3.08:1 when RPO Z22 Rally Sport option is ordered

** 3.07:1 when RPO Z22 Rally Sport option is ordered

Equipment Included with Optional V-8 Engines

275hp Turbo-Fire 327

Special front and rear springs*
Rear axle radius rod**
Rear axle ring gear 8.875in.**
Larger capacity radiator
Higher-performance starter

295hp Turbo-Fire 350

Special front and rear springs
Rear axle radius rod***
Rear axle ring gear 8.875in. diameter
Larger capacity radiator
Higher-performance starter
Heavier-duty driveshaft universal joints

Dual exhaust (2.25in) with resonators
Heavier-duty clutch
Red stripe nylon tires on 14x6 wheels
Special hood with simulated louvers****
Special chrome accents on motor

325hp Turbo-Jet 396

Special front and rear springs
Rear axle radius rod
Rear axle ring gear 8.875in. diameter
Larger capacity radiator
Higher-performance starter
Heavier-duty driveshaft universal joints
Dual exhaust (2.25in) with resonators
Heavier-duty clutch
Red stripe nylon tires on 14x6 wheels
Special hood with simulated louvers****
Special chrome accents on motor
Special shock absorbers
Special lower ball joints in front suspension
Heavier-duty engine mounts

* Convertible only
** Four-speed transmission only
*** Three- and four-speed transmissions only
**** Includes special under-hood insulation

1968 Power Teams

ENGINE	TRANSMISSION	REAR AXLE RATIO MODEL APPLICATION	REAR AXLE RATIO							
			Without air conditioning				With airconditioning			
			Std	Econ	Perf	Spec	Std	Edon	Perf	Spec
Standard 6 **140-hp Turbo-** **Thrift 230** **6-cylinder**	3-spd	All models	3.08	2.73	3.55		3.08		3.55	
	4-spd	All models	3.08	2.73	3.55		3.08		3.55	
	Powerglide	All models	2.73 *	2.56	3.55		3.08		3.55	
RPO L22 **155-hp Turbo-** **Thrift 250** **6-cylinder**	4-spd	All models	3.08	2.73	3.55		3.08		3.55	
	Powerglide	All models	2.73 *	2.56	3.55		3.08		3.55	
RPO Z28 **290-hp** **Turbo-Fire 302** **8-cylinder**	4-spd	Sport Coupe only	3.73		3.07 3.31	3.55 4.10 4.56 4.88	Air Conditioning Not Available			
Standard V8 **210-hp** **Turbo-Fire 327** **8-cylinder**	3-spd	All models	3.08	2.73	3.55		3.08		3.55	
	4-spd	All models	3.08	2.73	3.55		3.08		3.55	
	Powerglide	All models	2.73 *	2.56	3.55		3.08		3.55	
RPO L30 **275-hp** **Turbo-Fire 327** **8-cylinder**	3-spd	All models	3.08	2.73	3.55		3.08		3.55	
	4-spd	All models	3.07	2.73	3.55		3.07		3.55	
	Powerglide	All models	2.73 *	2.56	3.55		3.08		3.55	
RPO L48 **295-hp Turbo-Fire** **350** **8-cylinder**	3-spd	All models	3.31	3.07	3.55		3.31	3.07	3.55	
	Spec 3-spd	All models	3.31	3.07	3.55	3.73	3.31	3.07	3.55	
	4-spd	All models	3.31	3.07	3.55	3.73.1**	3.31	3.07	3.55	
	Powerglide	All models	3.07	2.73	3.31	3.55 3.73	3.07	2.73	3.31	
RPO L35 **325-hp Turbo-** **Jet 396** **8-cylinder**	Spec 3-spd	All models	3.07	2.73	3.31		3.07	2.73	3.31	
	4-spd	All models	3.07	2.73	3.31		3.07	2.73	3.31	
	Turbo HM	All models	2.73 ***	2.56	3.07		2.73 ***		3.07	
RPO L34 **350 hp Turbo-** **Jet 396** **Avail w/Camaro** **SS RPO Z27 only**	Special 3-spd MC1	12437/12467	3.31	3.07	3.55	3.73	3.31	3.07	3.55	3.73
	4-spd	12437/12467	3.31	3.07	3.55	3.73 *	3.31	3.07	3.55	3.73
	3-spd Auto	12437/12467	3.07	2.73	3.31	3.55 **	3.07	2.73	3.31	3.55 ***
RPO L78 **375 hp Turbo-** **Jet 396** **Avail w/Camaro** **SS RPO Z27 only**	Special 3-spd MC1	12437/12467	3.55	3.31	3.73		Air Conditioning Not Available			
	4-spd	12437/12467	3.55	3.31	3.73	3.07 *				
	3-spd Auto	12437/12467	3.31	3.07	3.55	3.73				
RPO L78/L89 **375 hp Turbo-** **Jet 396** **Avail w/Camaro** **SS RPO Z27 only**	Special 3-spd MC1	12437/12467	3.55	3.31	3.73		Air Conditioning Not Available			
	4-spd	12437/12467	3.55	3.31	3.73	3.07 *	*-also in 4.10			
	3-spd Auto	12437/12467	3.31	3.07	3.55	3.73 *	**-also in 3.73 and 4.10			

RPO L34 **350 hp Turbo-** **Jet 396** **Avail w/Camaro** **SS RPO Z27 only**	Special 3-spd MC1 4-spd 3-spd Auto	12437/12467 12437/12467 12437/12467	3.31 3.31 3.07	3.07 3.07 2.73	3.55 3.55 3.31	3.73 3.73 * 3.55 **	3.31 3.31 3.07	3.07 3.07 2.73	3.55 3.73 3.55 3.73 3.31 3.55 ***
RPO L78 **375 hp Turbo-** **Jet 396** **Avail w/Camaro** **SS RPO Z27 only**	Special 3-spd MC1 4-spd 3-spd Auto	12437/12467 12437/12467 12437/12467	3.55 3.55 3.31	3.31 3.31 3.07	3.73 3.73 3.55	 3.07 * 3.73	Air Conditioning Not Available		
RPO L78/L89 **375 hp Turbo-** **Jet 396** **Avail w/Camaro** **SS RPO Z27 only**	Special 3-spd MC1 4-spd 3-spd Auto	12437/12467 12437/12467 12437/12467	3.55 3.55 3.31	3.31 3.31 3.07	3.73 3.73 3.55	 3.07 * 3.73 *	Air Conditioning Not Available *-also in 4.10 **-also in 3.73 and 4.10		

* Also with Rally Sport
** Also available in 4.10:1 posi, 4.56:1 posi, and 4.88:1 posi
*** 3.07:1 with Rally Sport

1968 Camaro Transmissions

A fully synchronized three-speed transmission was installed in both six-cylinder engines and the 327/210, 327/275, and 350/295 eight-cylinder engines. Gear ratios for the six-cylinders were 1st - 2.85, 2nd - 1.68, 3rd - 1.00, and reverse - 2.95. The eight-cylinder machines' gear ratios were 1st - 2.54, 2nd - 1.50, 3rd - 1.00, and a 2.63 reverse. These transmissions were available in column, floor, or console shift.

RPO M13 consisted of a special three-speed fully synchronized transmission and was available on the 350/295 and 396/325 eight-cylinder engines. First gear was 2.41, 2nd - 1.59, 3rd - 1.00, and 2.41 reverse. These were available on the column or console.

RPO M20, a fully synchronized four-speed, was available on both six-cylinder engines with a 2.85 first gear, 2.02 second, 1.35 third, and 1.00 fourth, and 2.85 reverse. Gear ratios on the 327/210 and 327/275 engines were 1rst - 2.54, 2nd - 1.80, 34d - 1.44, 4th - 1.00, and 2.54 reverse. On the 250/295 and the 396/325 eight-cylinders gear ratios were 2.52 first, 1.88 second, 1.46 third, 1.00 fourth, and 2.59 reverse. This transmission was available with floor or console shift.

The M35 Powerglide was available on the column or console-shifted. It was available on both six-cylinder engines as well as the 327/210, 327/285, and 350/295 eight-cylinder engines.

The Turbo Hydra-matic (RPO M40) was available on the 396/325 in column, floor, or console shift.

Clutches

Both six-cylinder models utilized a diaphragm spring type 9.12in diameter clutch with a 1650–1850lb pressure plate. All V-8s used a semi-centrifugal bent finger design, diaphragm type clutch. The 327/210 and 327/275 models had a 10.40in diameter clutch with a 2100–2300lb pressure plate. The 11in clutch was used on the 350/295 and 396/325 models.

Equipment Included with Optional V-8 Engines

The 327/275 Turbo-Fire V-8 included special front springs, larger capacity radiator, heavier duty clutch, and higher-performance starter. When ordered with four-speed transmission, it also included special multi-leaf rear springs, heavier duty driveshaft universal joints, engine mounts, clutch, and starter, 8.875in ring gear, larger capacity radiator, 2.25in dual exhaust, red stripe wide-oval tires on 14x6 wheels, special hood with simulated louvers and insulation, chrome finish air cleaner, valve covers, and oil filler cap.

1969 Power Teams

ENGINE	TRANSMIS-SION	REAR AXLE RATIO MODEL APPLICATION	REAR AXLE RATIO							
			Without air conditioning				With airconditioning			
			Std	Econ	Perf	Spec	Std	Edon	Perf	Spec
Standard 6	3-speed (2.85 low)	All models	3.08	2.73	3.36		3.08	2.73	3.36	
145 hp Turbo-	4-speed (2.85 low)	All models	3.08	2.73	3.36		3.08	2.73	3.36	
Thrift 230	Torque-Drive	All models	2.73	2.56	3.08	3.36	3.08	2.73	3.36	
230 cu in Six	Powerglide	All models	2.73	2.56	3.08	3.36	3.08	2.73	3.36	
	Turbo Hydramatic	All models	2.56		2.73	3.08 3.36	2.73	2.56	3.08	3.36
RPO L22	3-spd (2.85 low)	All models	3.08	2.73	3.36		3.08	2.73	3.36	
155 hp Turbo-	4-speed (2.85 low)	All models	3.08	2.73	3.36		3.08	2.73	3.36	
Thrift 230	Torque-Drive	All models	2.73	2.56	3.08	3.36	3.08	2.73	3.36	
230 cu in Six	Powerglide	All models	2.73	2.56	3.08	3.36	3.08	2.73	3.36	
	Turbo Hydramatic	All models	2.56		2.73	3.08 3.36	2.73	2.56	3.08	3.36
Standard V8	3-speed (2.85 low)	All models	3.08	2.73	3.36		3.08		3.36	
200 hp Turbo-Fire	4-speed (2.85 low)	All models	3.08	2.73	3.36		3.08		3.36	
307	Powerglide	All models	2.73	2.56	3.08		2.73			3.36
307 cu in V8	Turbo Hydramatic	All models	2.56		2.73		2.73		3.08	
(added 1/69)										
Standard V8	3-speed (2.54 low)	All models	3.08	2.73	3.36		3.08	2.73	3.36	
210 hp Turbo-Fire	4-speed (2.54 low)	All models	3.08	2.73	3.36		3.08	2.73	3.36	
327	Powerglide	All models	2.73	2.56		3.36	2.73	2.56		3.36
327 cu in V8	Turbo Hydramatic	All models	2.73	2.56		3.36	2.73	2.56		3.36
(deleted 1/69)										
RPO LM1	Special 3-speed (2.42 low)	All models	3.31	3.07	3.55	3.73 *	3.31	3.07	3.55	3.73 *
255 hp Turbo-Fire 350	4-speed (2.52 low)	All models	3.31	3.07	3.55	3.73 *	3.31	3.07	3.55	3.73 *
350 cu in V8	Powerglide	All models	3.08	2.73	3.36	3.55	3.08	2.73	3.36	3.55
(dropped during production)	Turbo Hydramatic	All models	3.08	2.73	3.36	3.55	3.08	2.73	3.36	3.55
RPO L65	3-speed (2.54 low)	All models	3.08	2.73	3.36		3.08	2.73	3.36	
250 hp Turbo-Fire	4-speed (2.54 low)	All models	3.08	2.73	3.36		3.08	2.73	3.36	
350	Powerglide	All models	2.56			3.08	2.56			3.08
350 cu in V8	Turbo Hydramatic	All models	2.56			3.08	2.56			3.08
(added during production)										
300 hp Turbo-Fire 350	Special 3-speed (2.43 low)	All models	3.31	3.07	3.55	3.73 *	3.31	3.07	3.55	3.73 *
350 cu in V8	4-speed (2.52 low)	All models	3.31	3.07	3.55	3.73 * 4.10 *	3.31	3.07	3.55	3.73 *
Included with Ca-maro SS Equip-	Powerglide	All models	3.08		3.36		3.08		3.36	
ment (RPO Z27)	Turbo Hydramatic	All models	3.07	2.73	3.31	3.55	3.07	2.73	3.31	3.55

* Available as posi-traction axle only

146

ENGINE	TRANSMISSION	REAR AXLE RATIO MODEL APPLICATION	REAR AXLE RATIO Without air conditioning				With airconditioning			
			Std	Econ	Perf	Spec	Std	Edon	Perf	Spec
RPO L35 **325 hp Turbo-Jet 396** **396 cu in V8** **Avail w/Camaro SS (RPO Z27) only**	Special 3-speed (2.42 low)	All models	3.07	2.73	3.31		3.07	2.73	3.31	
	4-speed (2.52 low)	All models	3.07	2.73	3.31		3.07	2.73	3.31	
	Turbo Hydramatic	All models	3.07	2.73		2.56	3.07	2.73		2.56
RPO L34 **350 hp Turbo-Jet 396** **396 cu in V8** **Avail w/Camaro SS (RPO Z27) only**	Special 3-speed (MC1)	12437/12467	3.31	3.07	3.55	3.73	3.31	3.07	3.55	3.73
	4-speed wide-range M20	12437/12467	3.31	3.07	3.55	3.73	3.31	3.07	3.55	3.73
	4-speed close-ratio M21	12437/12467				3.73	3.31	3.07	3.55	3.73
			3.31	3.07	3.55	4.10				
	3-speed Auto M40	12437/12467	3.07	2.73	3.31	3.55 3.73 4.10	3.07	2.73	3.31	3.55 or 3.73
RPO L78 **375 hp Turbo-Jet 396** **396 cu in V8** **Avail w/Camaro SS (RPO Z27) only**	Special 3-speed (MC1)	12437/12467	3.55	3.31	3.73		Air Conditioning Not Available			
	4-speed wide-range M20	12437/12467	3.55	3.31	3.73	3.07 4.10				
	4-speed close-ratio M21	12437/12467	3.35	3.31	3.73	3.07 4.10				
	HD 4-speed close-ratio M22	12437/12467	3.55	3.31	3.73	3.07 4.10				
	3-speed auto M40	12437/12467	3.31	3.07	3.55	3.73 4.10				
RPO L78/L89 **375 hp Turbo-Jet 396** **396 cu in V8** **Avail w/Camaro SS (Z27) only**	Special 3-speed MC1	12437/12467	3.55	3.31	3.73		Air Conditioning Not Available			
	4-speed close-ratio M21	12437/12467	3.55	3.31	3.73	3.07 4.10				
	HD 4-speed close-ratio M22	12437/12467	3.55	3.31	3.73	3.07 4.10				
	3-speed automatic M40	12437/12467	3.31	3.07	3.55	3.73 4.10				
RPO Z28 **290 hp Turbo-Fire 302** **302 cu in V8**	4-speed wide-range M20	Model 12437	3.73	3.55	4.10	3.07 3.31	Air Conditioning Not Available			
	4-speed close-ratio M21	Only	3.73	3.55	4.10	3.07 3.31				
	HD 4-speed close-ratio M22		3.73	3.55	4.10	3.07 3.31				

ENGINE	TRANSMIS-SION	REAR AXLE MODEL APPLICATION	REAR AXLE RATIO							
			Without air conditioning				With airconditioning			
			Std	Econ	Perf	Spec	Std	Edon	Perf	Spec
COPO 9561 425 hp Turbo-Jet 427 V8 8-cylinder special cam large 4-bbl carb 11 compression mechanical lifters dual exhaust	4-speed close-ratio M21	12437 only	4.10				Unknown at this time if available			
	HD 4-speed close-ratio M22		4.10							
	3-speed automatic M40		4.10							
COPO 9560 430 hp Turbo-Jet 427 V8 aluminum block aluminum cyl heads special cam 12 compression mechanical lifters dual exhaust	4-speed close-ratio M21	12437 only	4.10				Unknown at this time if available			
	4-speed close-ratio M22		4.10							
	3-speed automatic M40		4.10							

Note: 9560 and 9561 options were not on the regular dealer order sheet!

Cubic In.	HP	Torque	Carb	Lifters	Comp.	Firing Order	Lash
230	140	220	1-bbl	H	8.5:1	1-5-3-6-2-4	1 TD from 0 lash
250	155	235	1-bbl	H	8.5:1	1-5-3-6-2-4	1 TD from 0 lash
302	290	290	4-bbl*	S	11:1	1-8-4-3-6-5-7-2	30–30
307	200	300	2-bbl	H	9:1	1-8-4-3-6-5-7-2	1 TD from 0 lash
327	210	320	2-bbl	H	9:1	1-8-4-3-6-5-7-2	1 TD from 0 lash
350	255	365	4-bbl	H	9:1	1-8-4-3-6-5-7-2	1 TD from 0 lash
350	300	380	4-bbl	H	10.25:1	1-8-4-3-6-5-7-2	1 TD from 0 lash
396	325	410	4-bbl	H	10.25:1	1-8-4-3-6-5-7-2	1 TD from 0 lash
396	350	415	4-bbl	H	10.25:1	1-8-4-3-6-5-7-2	1 TD from 0 lash
396	375	415	4-bbl*	S	11:1	1-8-4-3-6-5-7-2	024–28
427	425	460	4-bbl*	S	11:1	1-8-4-3-6-5-7-2	024–28
427	430	450	4-bbl*	S	12:1	1-8-4-3-6-5-7-2	022–24

*Holley carburetor on aluminum intake
TD - turndown
H - hydraulic
S - solid

1970 Power Teams

ENGINE	TRANSMISSION	MODEL APPLICATION	AXLE RATIO STD.	PERF
Turbo Thrift 250 250 cubic inch L-6 155 hp Standard	3-speed (2.85 low) Powerglide	All models	3.08 2.73	N/A N/A
Turbo Fire 307 307 cubic inch V-8 200 hp Standard	3-speed (2.85 low) Powerglide Turbo Hydra-Matic	All models	3.08 2.73 2.73	3.08 2.73 2.73
Turbo Fire 350 350 cubic inch V-8 250 hp RPO L65	4-speed (2.54 low) Turbo Hydra-Matic	All models	3.36 2.73	3.36 2.73
Turbo Fire 350 350 cubic inch V-8 300 hp RPO L48	4-speed (2.52 low) Turbo Hydra-Matic	All models	3.31 3.07	3.31 3.07
Turbo Fire 350 350 cubic inch V-8 360 hp RPO Z28	4-speed (2.52 low) 4-speed (2.20 low) HD 4-speed (2.20 low) Turbo Hydra-Matic	All models	3.73* 3.73* 3.73* 3.73*	NA NA NA NA
Turbo Jet 396 402 cubic inch V-8 350 hp RPO L34	4-speed (2.52 low) 4-speed (2.20 low) Turbo Hydra-Matic	All models	3.31 3.31 3.31	3.31 3.31 3.31

Posi-traction axles available optionally

1971 Power Teams

ENGINE	TRANSMISSION	MODEL APPLICATION	AXLE RATIO STD.	PERF
Turbo Thrift 250 250 cubic inch L-6 145 hp Standard	3-speed (2.85 low) Powerglide	All models	3.08 3.08	N/A N/A
Turbo Fire 307 307 cubic inch V-8 200 hp Standard	3-speed (2.85 low) Powerglide Turbo Hydra-Matic	All models	3.08 2.73 2.73	3.08 2.73 2.73
Turbo Fire 350 350 cubic inch V-8 245 hp RPO L65	4-speed (2.54 low) Turbo Hydra-Matic	All models	3.08 2.73	3.08 2.73
Turbo Fire 350 350 cubic inch V-8 270 hp RPO L48	4-speed (2.52 low) Turbo Hydra-Matic	All models	3.42 3.08	3.42 3.08
Turbo Fire 350 350 cubic inch V-8 330 hp RPO Z28	4-speed (2.52 low) 4-speed (2.20 low) HD 4-speed (2.20 low) Turbo Hydra-Matic	All models	3.73* 3.73* 3.73* 3.73*	NA NA NA NA
Turbo Jet 396 402 cubic inch V-8 300 hp RPO LS3	4-speed (2.52 low) 4-speed (2.20 low) Turbo Hydra-Matic	All models	3.42 3.42 3.42	3.42 3.42 3.42

1972 Power Teams

ENGINE	TRANSMISSION	MODEL APPLICATION	AXLE RATIO STD.	PERF
Turbo Thrift 250	3-speed (2.85 low)	All models	3.08	
250 cubic inch L-6	Powerglide		3.08	
155 hp Standard				
Turbo Fire 307	3-speed (2.85 low)	All models	3.08	
307 cubic inch V-8	Powerglide		2.73	
200 hp Standard	Turbo Hydra-Matic		2.73	
Turbo Fire 350	4-speed (2.54 low)	All models	3.08	
350 cubic inch V-8	Turbo Hydra-Matic		2.73	
RPO L65				
Turbo Fire 350	4-speed (2.42 low)	All models	3.42	
350 cubic inch V-8	Turbo Hydra-Matic		3.08	
RPO L48				
Turbo Fire 350	4-speed (2.52 low)	All models	3.73*	4.10
350 cubic inch V-8	4-speed (2.20 low)		3.73*	4.10
RPO Z28	HD 4-speed (2.20 low)		3.73*	4.10
	Turbo Hydra-Matic		3.73*	4.10
Turbo Jet 396	4-speed (2.52 low)	All models	3.42	
402 cubic inch V-8	4-speed (2.20 low)		3.42	
RPO LS3	Turbo Hydra-Matic		3.42	

Posi-traction axles available optionally

1973 Power Teams

ENGINE	TRANSMISSION	MODEL APPLICATION	AXLE RATIO STD.	PERF
Turbo Thrift 250	3-speed (2.85 low)	1FQ87 only	3.08	
250 cubic inch L-6	Turbo Hydra-Matic		3.08	
Standard				
Turbo Fire 307	3-speed (2.85 low)	1FQ87 only	3.08	
307 cubic inch V-8	Turbo Hydra-Matic		2.73	
RPO L14				
Turbo Fire 350	3-speed (2.54 low)	All models	3.08	
350 cubic inch V-8	4-speed (2.54 low)#	(Standard 1FS87)		
RPO L65	Turbo Hydra-Matic		2.73	
Turbo Fire 350	3-speed (2.54 low)	All models	3.42	
350 cubic inch V-8	4-speed (2.54 low)			
RPO L48	Turbo Hydra-Matic		3.08	
Turbo Fire 350	4-speed (2.52 low)	All models	3.73*	
350 cubic inch V-8	4-speed (2.20 low)		3.73*	
RPO Z28	Turbo Hydra-Matic		3.73*	

Posi-traction axles available optionally

Miscellaneous Dated Parts

Alternator
Example: 8C7
8 - Year
C - Month
7 - Date
Year:
6 - 1966
7 - 1967
8 - 1968
9 - 1969
0 - 1970
1 - 1971
2 - 1972
3 - 1973

Month:
A - January
B - February
C - March
D - April
E - May
F - June
G - July
H - August
J - September
K - October
L - November
M - December

Date:
01-31 Day of Month

Carburetor, Holley
Example: 841
8 - Year
4 - Month
1 - Week

Year:
6 - 1966
7 - 1967
8 - 1968
9 - 1969
0 - 1970
1 - 1971
2 - 1972
3 - 1973

Month:
1 - January
2 - February
3 - March
4 - April
5 - May
6 - June
7 - July
8 - August
9 - September
0 - October
N - November
D - December

Week:
1 - 1st week of month
2 - 2nd week of month
3 - 3rd week of month
4 - 4th week of month
5 - 5th week of month

Carpet
Example: 4/21/68
4 - Month
21 - Date
68 - Year

Month:
1 - January
2 - February
3 - March
4 - April
5 - May
6 - June
7 - July
8 - August
9 - September
10 - October
11 - November
12 - December

Date:
01-31 Date of Month

Year:
66 - 1966
67 - 1967
68 - 1968
69 - 1969
70 - 1970
71 - 1971
72 - 1972
73 - 1973
This information was taken from J.P. Stevens supplied carpet. Other supplies may have used different coding.

Cylinder Heads
Example: E28
E - Month
2 - Day
8 - Year

Dated Holley carburetor.

Month:
A - January
B - February
C - March
D - April
E - May
F - June
G - July
H - August
I - September
J - October
K - November
L - December

Day:
1-31

Year:
6 - 1966
7 - 1967
8 - 1968
9 - 1969

0 - 1970
1 - 1971
2 - 1972
3 - 1973

Distributor
Example: 8A15
8 - Year
A - Month
15 - Day

Year:
6 - 1966
7 - 1967
8 - 1968
9 - 1969
0 - 1970
1 - 1971
2 - 1972
3 - 1973

Month:
A - January
B - February
C - March
D - April
E - May
F - June
G - July
H - August
J - September
K - October
L - November
M - December

Day:
01-31

**Engine Block
Assembly Date**
Example: V0512MO
V - Plant (see Protect-O-
Plate information)

05 - Month
12 - Date
MO - Suffix (see Protect-O-Plate information)

Month:
01 - January
02 - February
03 - March
04 - April
05 - May
06 - June
07 - July
08 - August
09 - September
10 - October
11 - November
12 - December

Date:
01-31

Engine Block Casting Date
Example: D288
D - Month
28 - Date
8 - Year

Month:
A - January
B - February
C - March
D - April
E - May
F - June
G - July
H - August
I - September
J - October
K - November
L - December

Date:
01-31

Year:
6 - 1966
7 - 1967
8 - 1968
9 - 1969
0 - 1970
1 - 1971
2 - 1972

3 - 1973

Exhaust Manifolds
Example: D188
D - Month
18 - Date
8 - Year

Month:
A - January
B - February
C - March
D - April
E - May
F - June
G - July
H - August
I - September
J - October
K - November
L - December

Date:
01-31

Year:
6 - 1966
7 - 1967
8 - 1968
9 - 1969
0 - 1970
1 - 1971
2 - 1972
3 - 1973

Flywheel
Example: D18
D - Month
1 - Date
8 - Year

Month:
A - January
B - February
C - March
D - April
E - May
F - June
G - July
H - August
I - September
J - October
K - November
L - December

Date:
01-31

Year:
6 - 1966
7 - 1967
8 - 1968
9 - 1969
0 - 1970
1 - 1971
2 - 1972
3 - 1973

Glass
Example: J X
J - Month
X - Year

Month:
N - January
X - February
L - March
G - April
J - May
I - June
U - July
T - August
A - September
Y - October
C - November
V - December

Year:
Z - 1967
X - 1968
V - 1969
T - 1970

Headrests
Example: 1 68
1 - Month
68 - Year

Month:
1 - January
2 - February
3 - March
4 - April
5 - May
6 - June
7 - July
8 - August
9 - September
10 - October

11 - November
12 - December

Year:
67 - 1967
68 - 1968
69 - 1969
70 - 1970
We have seen some head-rests coded with month, day, and year (1-15-69).

Intake Manifold
Example: 101368
10 - Month
13 - Date
68 - Year
Month:
1 - January
2 - February
3 - March
4 - April
5 - May
6 - June
7 - July
8 - August
9 - September
10 - October
11 - November
12 - December

Date:
1-31

Year:
66 - 1966
67 - 1967
68 - 1968
69 - 1969
70 - 1970
71 - 1971
72 - 1972
73 - 1973

Jack
The jack was coded with the year on the base and load rest bracket. The rivet where wrench was inserted contained the month and year.

Mirror
Example: 11DMI68

11 - Month
DMI - Manufacturer (Don-nelly Mirror, Inc.)
68 - Year

Month:
1 - January
2 - February
3 - March
4 - April
5 - May
6 - June
7 - July
8 - August
9 - September
10 - October
11 - November
12 - December

Year:
66 - 1966
67 - 1967
68 - 1968
69 - 1969
70 - 1970
71 - 1971
72 - 1972
73 - 1973

Plastic Window, Convertible
Example: 13H68
13 - Day
H - Month
68 - Year

Day:
1-31

Month:
A - January
B - February
C - March
D - April
E - May
F - June
G - July
H - August
I - September
J - October
K - November
L - December

Year:
66 - 1966
67 - 1967
68 - 1968
69 - 1969
70 - 1970

Radiator
The radiator is coded by year on the tag which is located on the side of the radiator

Rear Axle Assembly Date
Example: QX519G2
QX - Ratio (see Protect-O-Plate information)
5 - Month
19 - Date
G - Gear Plant (see Pro-tect-O-Plate information)
2 - Shift

Month:
01 - January
02 - February
03 - March
04 - April
05 - May
06 - June
07 - July
08 - August
09 - September
10 - October
11 - November
12 - December

Date:
01-31

Shift:
1 - 1st shift
2 - 2nd shift

Rear Housing Casting Date
Example: A18
A - Month
1 - Date
8 - Year

Month:
A - January
B - February

C - March
D - April
E - May
F - June
G - July
H - August
I - September
J - October
K - November
L - December

Date:
1-31

Year:
6 - 1966
7 - 1967
8 - 1968
9 - 1969
0 - 1970
1 - 1971
2 - 1972
3 - 1973

Replacement Battery
The year is found on the warranty card included with battery

Ring and Pinion Gear
Example: 1 68
1 - Month
68 - Year

Month:
1 - January
2 - February
3 - March
4 - April
5 - May
6 - June
7 - July
8 - August
9 - September
10 - October
11 - November
12 - December

Year:
66 - 1966
67 - 1967
68 - 1968
69 - 1969
70 - 1970

Engine block assembly date.

71 - 1971
72 - 1972
73 - 1973

Seat Belts
Example: 7A68
7 - Week
A - Manufacturer
68 - Year
Week:
1-52 Week of Year

Year:
66 - 1966
67 - 1967
68 - 1968
69 - 1969
70 - 1970
71 - 1971
72 - 1972
73 - 1973

Shocks
Original shocks are date with the year, yet other codes appear also.

Spark Plug Wires
Example: 1Q68
1 - Quarter
Q - Quarter
68 - Year
Quarter:

1-3 - 1st Quarter of Year
4-6 - 2nd Quarter of Year
7-9 - 3rd Quarter of Year
10-12 - 4th Quarter of Year
Year:
66 - 1966
67 - 1967
68 - 1968
69 - 1969
70 - 1970
71 - 1971
72 - 1972
73 - 1973

Starter
Example: 8E14
8 - Year
E - Month
14 - Date

Year:
6 - 19660 - 1970
7 - 19671 - 1971
8 - 19682 - 1972
9 - 19693 - 1973

Month:
A - January
B - February
C - March
D - April
E - May

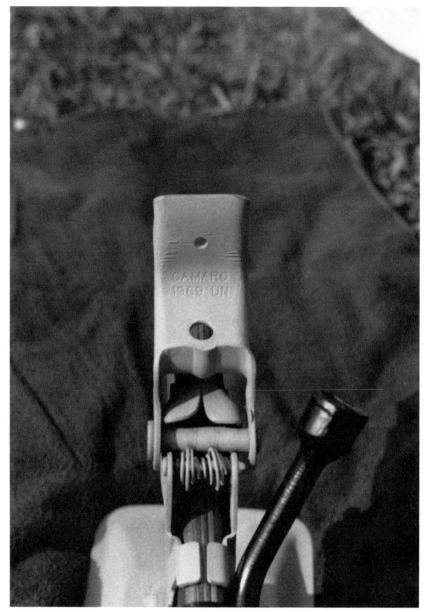
Dated jack assembly.

2 - February
3 - March
4 - April
5 - May
6 - June
7 - July
8 - August
9 - September
10 - October
11 - November
12 - December

Year:
66 - 1966
67 - 1967
68 - 1968
69 - 1969
70 - 1970
71 - 1971
72 - 1972
73 - 1973

Transmission Assembly
Example: P8R13
P - Type (see Protect-O-Plate information)
8 - Year
R - Month
13 - Date

Year:
6 - 1966
7 - 1967
8 - 1968
9 - 1969
0 - 1970
1 - 1971
2 - 1972
3 - 1973

Month:
A - January
B - February
C - March
D - April
E - May
H - June
K - July
M - August
P - September
R - October
S - November
T - December

F - June
G - July
H - August
I - September
J - October
K - November
L - December

Date:
1-31

Timing Cover
Original small block timing covers, and possibly big block, have been seen with date codes.

Top Boot
Top boots manufactured by Firestone were date coded with the month, day, and year.

Tower Clamp
Example: 1 68
1 - Month
68 - Year
Month:
1 - January

Date:
1-31
Often transmission would have a number or letter after the date which would indicate the shift. Those codes are as follows:
1 - 1st shift
2 - 2nd shift
A - 1st shift
B - 2nd shift
D - Day (1st shift)
N - Night (2nd shift)

Voltage Regulator
Example: 8 A
8 - Year
A - Month

Year:
6 - 1966
7 - 1967
8 - 1968
9 - 1969
0 - 1970
1 - 1971
2 - 1972
3 - 1973

Month:
A - January
B - February
C - March
D - April
E - May
F - June
G - July
H - August
I - September
J - October
K - November
L - December

Water Pump
Example: B288
B - Month
28 - Date
8 - Year

Month:
A - January
B - February
C - March
D - April

E - May
F - June
G - July
H - August
I - September
J - October
K - November
L - December

Date:
01-31

Year:
6 - 1966
7 - 1967
8 - 1968
9 - 1969
0 - 1970
1 - 1971
2 - 1972
3 - 1973

Wheels
Example: K188
K - Manufacturer (Kelsey Hayes)
1 - Use Code (Chevrolet)
8 - Year
8 - Month

Year:
6 - 1966
7 - 1967
8 - 1968
9 - 1969
0 - 1970
1 - 1971
2 - 1972
3 - 1973

Month:
1 - January
2 - February
3 - March
4 - April
5 - May
6 - June
7 - July
8 - August
9 - September
10 - October
11 - November
12 - December
Next to the valve stem another

number would be found. This would indicate the day of the month. These should run from 1-31.

Wiper Motor
The wiper motor is date coded.

Component Finishes
Chevrolet Orange
Engine block including oil pan (the number pad was not painted)
Harmonic balancer
Water pump
Heads (except aluminum heads)
Valve covers (except big block and Z28)
Bell housing received orange overspray
Exhaust manifolds received orange overspray
ZL1 block remained natural along with cylinder heads
Oil pan, timing cover, and water pump were painted black

Semi-Flat Black Paint
Air conditioning compressor and supports
Fender wells
Firewall
License plate brackets
Master cylinder
Pedal supports
Sway bar brackets

Gloss Black Paint
Air cleaner and base
Alternator bracket
Harmonic balancer pulley (except big block)
Coil
Engine fan
PCV tube from back of block
Power steering pump and brackets
Radiator
Voltage regulator cover
Water pump pulley
Wheels (except rally wheels)

Unpainted/Unplated Finishes

Bail wires
Balancer pulley on the big block
Clutch return spring connecting rod
Copper ground straps
Dipstick handles
Front and rear springs
Fuel and brake lines
Rear end (housings appear to have come in plain, black, and bottom black-top plain)
Sway bar
Center link
Tie rod ends
Adjusting sleeves
Throw out fork (orange overspray on fork)

Black Oxide

Bell housing bolts
Bumper brackets (front and rear)
Distributor hold-down clamp
Exhaust manifold bolts
Fender bolts
Hood pin spring
PCV hose clamps
Transmission cross-member
Water pump bolts
Heater hose snap clamps (also red)

Gray Phosphate

The gray phosphate ranged in color from light to very dark.
Accelerator rod and lever
Accelerator spring and linkage
Clutch cross shaft and clutch linkage
Clutch return spring
Hood hinges and springs
Hood latch

Plated

Alternator, air conditioning, and smog pump mounting bolts
Alternator fan
Alternator (high performance) pulleys
Choke cover
Distributor vacuum pot
Fuel tank
Gas cap
Hose clamps
Jack post
Windshield washer nozzles

Cadmium Dichromate Plated

Master cylinder cover
Power brake booster
Smog pump valves
Proportioning valve support bracket

Gray Painted

Jack adapter, mechanism, and base
Shock absorbers
Space saver spare tire rim

Underbody of Car

The underbody appears to have received black or gray primer. We have also seen some cars with a light body color paint. Under the trunk area, the car received the exterior body color. Under the hood area was painted black. The subframe received semi-gloss black paint.

Index

1967 Camaro Exterior Color & Interior Trim Chart, 134
1967 Camaro Options, 8
1967 Camaro Protect-O-Plate, 14
1967 Camaro Regular Equipment Exterior, 6
1967 Camaro Regular Equipment Interior, 8
1967 Camaro Trim Plate, 13
1967 Engine Codes, 15
1967 Exterior Colors, 15
1967 Interior Colors, 14
1967 Manufacturer's suggested retail price (MSRP), 4
1967 Power Teams, 142
1968 Camaro Exterior Color & Interior Trim Chart, 135
1968 Camaro Exterior, 32
1968 Camaro Interior, 28
1968 Camaro Performance Options, 30
1968 Camaro Protect-O-Plate, 40
1968 Camaro Transmissions, 145
1968 Camaro Trim Plate, 39
1968 Exterior Colors, 40
1968 Interior Colors, 40
1968 Manufacturer's suggested retail price (MSRP), 24
1968 Power Teams, 144
1969 Camaro Exterior Color & Interior Trim Chart, 136
1969 Camaro Exterior, 48
1969 Camaro Features—Exterior, 47
1969 Camaro Features—Interior, 47
1969 Camaro Interior, 49
1969 Camaro Options, 51
1969 Camaro Protect-O-Plate, 61
1969 Camaro Trim Plate, 58
1969 Manufacturers suggested retail price (MSRP), 44
1969 Mid-Year Options, 56
1969 Power Teams, 146
1969 Production Statistics, 47
1970 Camaro Exterior Color & Interior Trim Chart, 137
1970 Camaro Exterior, 75
1970 Camaro Options, 81
1970 Camaro Protect-O-Plate, 84
1970 Camaro Specifications, 80
1970 Camaro Standard Equipment, 78
1970 Camaro Trim Plate, 84
1970 Manufacturer's suggested retail price (MSRP), 72
1970 Power Teams, 149
1971 Camaro Exterior Color & Interior Trim Chart, 138
1971 Camaro Options, 98
1971 Camaro Protect-O-Plate, 102
1971 Camaro Standard Equipment Exterior, 91

1971 Camaro Standard Equipment Interior, 94
1971 Camaro Trim Plate, 101
1971 Manufacturer's suggested retail price (MSRP) for base model Camaros, 89
1971 Power Teams, 149
1972 Camaro Exterior Color & Interior Trim Chart, 138
1972 Camaro Options, 112
1972 Camaro Protect-O-Plate, 117
1972 Camaro Standard Equipment Exterior, 106
1972 Camaro Standard Equipment Interior, 108
1972 Camaro Trim Plate, 116
1972 Engine Codes, 117
1972 Manufacturer's suggested retail price (MSRP), 104
1972 Power Teams, 150
1973 Camaro Exterior Color & Interior Trim Chart, 140
1973 Camaro Options & Accessories, 129
1973 Camaro Protect-O-Plate, 133
1973 Camaro Standard Equipment Exterior, 122
1973 Camaro Standard Equipment Interior, 124
1973 Camaro Trim Plate, 131
1973 Manufacturer's suggested retail price (MSRP), 120
1973 Power Teams, 150
Alternator, 151
Assemble Plants, 5
Assembly Plant, 13
Assembly Plant, 84
Assembly Plant, 101
Assembly Plant, 116
Assembly Plant, 131
Assembly Plants, 26
Assembly Plants, 90
Axle Ratios, 9
Basic Specifications, 5
Body Color, 59
Body Paint Code, 84
Body Paint Code, 101
Body Paint Code, 116
Body Paint Code, 132
Body Paint, 39
Body Style, 39
Body Style, 84
Body Style, 101
Body Style, 131
Body Unit Number, 13
Build Date Code, 84
Build Date Code, 101
Build Date Code, 116

Build Date Code, 132
Build Date, 13
Build Date, 39
Camaro Data Book Indexing
Camaro SS with 250 V-8, 29
Camaro SS with 396 V-8, 29
Camaro Standard Equipment, 24
Camaro Standard Equipment, 44
Camaro Standard Equipment, 72
Camaro Standard Equipment, 89
Camaro Standard Equipment, 104
Camaro Standard Equipment, 120
Carburetor Source, 15
Carburetor Source, 40
Carburetor Source, 85
Carburetor Source, 102
Carburetor Source, 117
Carburetor, Holley, 151
Carpet, 151
Component Finishes, 157
Convertible Top Color Choices, 136
Cylinder Heads, 1512
Distributor, 152
Engine Block Assembly Date, 152
Engine Block Casting Date, 153
Engine Identification, 6
Engine Identification, 27
Engine Identification, 90
Engine Identification, 105
Engine Identification, 122
Engine Production Code, 15
Engine Production Code, 40
Engine Production Code, 85
Engine Production Code, 102
Engine Production Code, 117
Engines, 9
Exhaust Manifolds, 153
Exterior Features, 9
Exterior Paint Processes, 141
Flywheel, 153
Headrests, 153
Intake Manifold, 154
Interior Color Code, 13
Interior Features, 10
Interior Trim Code, 58
Interior Trim Code, 84
Interior Trim Code, 101
Interior Trim Code, 116
Interior Trim Code, 131
Jack, 154
Lower Body Color, 13
Mirror, 154
Model Identification, 58
Model Year, 13
Model Year, 39
Month of Vehicle Build, 102
Month of Vehicle Build, 119
New Features for 1972, 111
New Features for 1973, 127
Option Code, 101
Option Code, 116
Option Code, 132
Plant Codes, 17
Plastic Window, Convertible, 154
Power Assists, 9

Radiator, 154
Rally Sport Package, 28
Rear Axle Assembly Date, 154
Rear Axle Code, 17
Rear Axle Code, 41
Rear Axle Code, 85
Rear Axle Code, 102
Rear Axle Code, 119
Rear Axle Identification, 6
Rear Axle Identification, 27
Rear Axle Identification, 75
Rear Axle Identification, 91
Rear Axle Identification, 106
Rear Housing Casting Date, 154
Replacement Battery, 155
Ring & Pinion Gear, 155
RS & SS Options, 29
Seat & Shoulder Belt Colors, 136
Seat Belts, 155
Semi-Flat Black Paint, 157
Serial Numbers & Identification Vehicle Identification Number
    (VIN), 4
Serial Numbers and Identification, 24
Serial Numbers Vehicle Identification Number (VIN), 46
Serial Numbers Vehicle Identification Number (VIN), 74
Serial Numbers Vehicle Identification Number (VIN), 90
Serial Numbers Vehicle Identification Number (VIN), 105
Serial Numbers Vehicle Identification Number (VIN), 120
Shift, 154
Shocks, 155
Source Designation, 90
Spark Plug Wires, 155
Standard Interior, 31
Starter, 155
Time Built Code, 47
Time Built Code, 59
Timing Cover, 156
Top Boot, 156
Tower Clamp, 156
Transmission Assembly, 156
Transmission Code, 65
Transmission Identification, 5
Transmission Identification, 27
Transmission Identification, 74
Transmission Identification, 90
Transmission Identification, 105
Transmission Identification, 121
Transmission Number, 17
Transmission Number, 86
Transmission Number, 103
Transmission Number, 119
Transmissions, 9
Underbody of Car, 158
Unpainted/Unplated Finishes, 158
Upper Body Color, 13
Vehicle Identification Number, 40
Vehicle Identification Number, 84
Vehicle Identification Number, 102
Vehicle Identification Number, 117
Voltage Regulator, 157
Water Pump, 157
Wheels, 157
Wiper Motor, 157
Z28 Stripe Color, 117
Z28 Stripe Color, 132